see it places to see

Sydney Icons

Bondi Beach ❶ 4F-5F
This famous beach is a curved moon of white sand facing the Tasman Sea. There's sun, sand and some of Sydney's best restaurants and shopping on Bondi's Campbell Parade. So it's not surprising that it's packed out in summer. If you seek peace and quiet, take the coastal walk to Tamarama or Bronte (see p.59).

Luna Park ❶ 4D
Since opening in 1935, Luna Park has had a chequered history. It was forced to close in 1979 when a fire killed seven people. It finally

The Face at Luna Park

reopened in April 2004, retaining much of its 1930s charm. Entry is free, but you need to purchase ride tickets at the ticket office. *Open 11am-6pm Mon-Thu, 11am-11pm Fri, 10am-11pm Sat, 10am-6pm Sun. 1 Olympic Dr, Milsons Pt, T: 9922 6644, www.lunaparksydney.com*

Manly Beach ❶ 1E
This North Shore beach, a long stretch of white sand lined with huge Norfolk Pines, is relaxed and popular with surfers. Cross the 'corso' to get to the harbour and the bars, restaurants and shops.

Sydney Harbour Bridge ❷ 1E
The Harbour Bridge was designed by Dorman & Long, who built the 1,149-m (3,770-ft) long single-arch bridge from the ends using cable support and joining it in the middle. At 503 m (1,650 ft) high, ships can pass through uninterrupted. Find out more about its history and take in the views at the Pylon Lookout. If you feel like a challenge, try the Bridge Climb, during which you'll cross the bridge's arch to the summit – provided you pass the blood-alcohol test beforehand!
Pylon Lookout: *Adm. Open 10am-5pm daily. SE Pylon, Sydney Harbour Bridge (entrance Bridge Stairs on Cumberland St, The Rocks), T: 9240 1100, www.pylonlookout.com.au*
Bridge Climb: *Adm. 5 Cumberland St, The Rocks, T: 8274 7777, www.bridgeclimb.com.au*

View over Bondi Beach

CONTENTS

see it places to see	2
buy it places to shop	16
watch it places to be entertained	26
taste it places to eat and drink	36
know it practical information	46
directory hotel listings and more	56
speak it and **index**	62

Map references are denoted in the text ❶ Greater Sydney ❷ Central Sydney
❸ Darling Harbour ❹ Sydney Area ❺ CityRail ❻ Olympic Park (map ❶ index)

sydney places to see

Sydney is both Australia's gateway and one of the world's most beautiful cities, particularly when the sun shines – and it does most of the time. The city's harbour sparkles with the reflection of its brilliant blue sky, its celebrated beaches are gorgeous stretches of gold and its leafy parks are quiet green havens. And natural beauty is not the only thing this vibrant city has to offer; it has a long background of indigenous habitation and a rich colonial history of many different races flocking here. This melting pot of cultures has endowed Sydney with a diversity that's evident in everything, from its architecture to its people.

Sydney Olympic Park ❻

This 683-hectare (1,688-acre) park was built specifically for the 2000 Sydney Olympic Games. Its sports facilities are still heavily utilised and include the ANZ Stadium, which has since held many major events including the Rugby World Cup finals in 2003. The Aquatic Centre nearby features two 50-m (164-ft) pools.

The Olympic Cauldron is located between the ANZ Stadium and the park's main train station. There, the names of thousands of Olympic and Paralympic medal-winning athletes are inscribed in the pavement around the cauldron which stands 10 m (33 ft) tall on 24 columns.

Olympic Park: *Open 9am-5pm daily. Tours available. Visitors Centre, 1 Showground Rd, Sydney Olympic Pk, T: 9714 7888, www.sydneyolympicpark.com.au*

ANZ Stadium: *Tours available. Open 10am-4pm daily. Edwin Flack Ave, Sydney Olympic Pk, T: 8765 2000, www.anzstadium.com.au*

Aquatic Centre: *Adm. Open 5am-9pm Mon-Fri, 6am-7pm Sat-Sun. Olympic Blvd, Sydney Olympic Pk, T: 9752 3666, www.aquaticcentre.com.au*

Sydney Opera House ❷ 2F

Photographs just don't do justice to this masterpiece of modern architecture. Designed in 1957 by Danish architect Jørn Utzon, more than a million white tiles cover huge vaulted shells, enclosing five performance spaces (*see p.29*). It was

> ### Time Out
> Take a break from the lunacy of Luna Park (*see p.4*) in Quiberie Park (❶ 4C). Sit under the Sydney Harbour Bridge (*see p.4*), or take in the northerly harbour views from the bottom of Jeffery Street (❶ 4D). To escape Kings Cross (*see p.11*) head to Rushcutters Bay Park (❶ 4E, cnr New Beach and New S Head Rds) where the waves lap against the moored yachts. Nielsen Park (❶ 3F, entrance Greycliffe Ave, Vaucluse) is the perfect picnic spot after a visit to Vaucluse House (❶ 3E, *see p.13*). There's also a tiny beach, the Hermitage Foreshore (❶ 3E) walk and some panoramic harbour views.

Sydney Harbour Bridge

Sydney Opera House, Sydney Harbour

budgeted at A$7 million but instead cost a cool A$102 million and took 12 additional years to construct, finally opening in October 1973. Do the daily hour-long tour of the house or the two-hour Backstage Tour, and take a walk on the Broadwalk encircling it for stunning harbour views.

Box Office: *Open 9am-8.30pm Mon-Sat. T: 9250 7777.*
Tours: *Adm. Open 9am-5pm daily. T: 9250 7250, Bennelong Pt, www.sydneyoperahouse.com*

Areas & Sights

Chinatown ❸

Bright, neon lights and bustling, noisy restaurants dominate Sydney's little China, which used to be located at The Rocks (*see p.13*) until Sydney's Chinese community moved to what is now Haymarket. Wander through in the evening, when it really comes to life. Take the train to Central Station, or follow the signs from Darling Harbour (*see p.7*). *Haymarket.*

Circular Quay ❷ 3E

Circular Quay has been a maritime hub since the First Fleet (*see box, p.13*) landed here in 1788. It is primarily a jumping-off point for everywhere else in Sydney (ferries, buses and trains all stop here – *see pp.49-51*), but there are also several historical sites and art galleries in the neighbourhood.

Museum of Contemporary Art (MCA) ❷ 3E

Since 1991 this Art Deco structure has housed the MCA's fascinating contemporary art exhibitions of paintings, photographs, performances and installations by Australian and international artists. There is also a collection of traditional Aboriginal art from Ramingining in the Northern Territory. There is a quayside café for the peckish. *Open 10am-5pm daily. 140 George St, The Rocks (also accessible from Circular Quay side), T: 9245 2400, www.mca.com.au*

Museum of Sydney ❷ 3E

The Museum of Sydney, designed by

Denton Corker Marshall in 1995, stands on the remains of the first Government House, from which nine governors dished out authority until its demolition in 1846. The museum tells Sydney's story, including Aboriginal culture from 1788 through to modern times. It has a nice café that makes a perfect pit stop. *Adm. Open 9.30am-5pm daily. 57 Phillip St (cnr Phillip and Bridge Sts), Sydney, T: 9251 5988, www.hht.net.au/museums/mos*

> **Ticket Through Time**
> The Historic Houses Trust's 'Ticket Through Time' gives access to its 13 museums and properties. Established in 1980 to care for Vaucluse House (see p.13) and Elizabeth Bay House (see p.11), the trust has since taken on 11 more properties, including Hyde Park Barracks Museum, Museum of Sydney (see p.6), Susannah Place Museum and Government House (see p.10). The pass is valid for three months, costs A$30 per adult or A$60 for a family, and is available at any of the Trust's museums. T: 8239 2288, www.hht.net.au

City

Get around Sydney's Central Business District by CityRail (see p.50), getting off at Martin Place or Town Hall, or take the Light Rail (see p.50) or alternatively the futuristic Monorail (see p.50).

Australian Museum ❷ 5F
Australia's oldest museum has collected and documented the nation's natural history for more than 175 years. It sits on land once occupied by the indigenous Eora people from Sydney's southern regions. The museum's collection illustrates the diversity of the Eora and other indigenous cultures and includes Yidaki didgeridoo performances on Sundays. Have a look at the 'what's on' sign at the information desk for daily hour-long tour details. *Adm. Open 9.30am-5pm daily. 6 College St, Sydney, T: 9320 6000, www.amonline.net.au*

Darling Harbour ❸
Darling Harbour was known to early settlers as a peaceful bay rich with shellfish (hence the name of Cockle Bay). With the building of a steam mill in 1815, it became an industrial centre that eventually fell into disuse. Now it is a sprawling complex of shops, hotels, cafés, museums, gardens and themed attractions. *www.darlingharbour.com*

Hyde Park ❷ 5E
Office workers, tourists and pigeons seeking respite from Sydney's streets flock to this leafy oasis spanning four city blocks. The park encloses a giant chessboard (near St James station), the Archibald Fountain and, at the south end of the park, the ANZAC War Memorial. The fountain and ANZAC memorial, built in 1932, commemorate Australian and other Allied troops who died in World War I. Steer clear of the park at night as it could be dangerous and is known to be a haven for drunks

and drug addicts. *Between College & Elizabeth Sts, Sydney.*

National Maritime Museum ❸
With its indoor exhibits documenting international and domestic maritime history, this museum celebrates the sea. Outside, a fleet of historic vessels floats on Cockle Bay, including a replica of the *Endeavour*, the ship on which James Cook first sailed around the world. *Adm. for boarding ships. Open 9.30am-5pm daily. 2 Murray St, Darling Hbr, T: 9298 3777, www.anmm.gov.au*

Queen Victoria Building ❷ 5D
The Queen Victoria Market Building (or QVB), George McRae's Romanesque setting for the new central city market, officially opened in 1898. After many city council modifications, it was restored to all its former glory in 1986, with tiled floors, timber balustrades, an original 19th-century staircase and stained-glass windows. The huge copper-sheathed glass dome now shelters a shopping mall, various public exhibits and a restored

tearoom on level three. A bronze Queen Victoria stands at the Druitt Street entrance. *Tours available. Open 9am-6pm Mon-Wed, Fri & Sat, 9am-9pm Thu, 11am-5pm Sun. Cnr George, Market, York and Druitt Sts, Town Hall, T: 9264 9209, www.qvb.com.au*

St Mary's Cathedral ❷ 5F
The beautiful St Mary's Cathedral is one of the largest cathedrals in the world. Completed in 1882, it is most famous for its mosaic-tiled crypt depicting the Creation. Free tours of the cathedral start at noon on Sundays. **Crypt:** *Open 10am-4pm daily. St Mary's Rd (opposite Hyde Pk),*

Aboriginal Sydney
Aboriginal people have lived in New South Wales for more than 40,000 years. The British colonial influx from the late 18th century brought with it disease, including smallpox and venereal disease epidemics, as well as the assimilation of Aboriginal children into white families until the 1960s and land lost to settlers. Despite all this, their rich culture remains. For a history lesson of the country, head to the Art Gallery of New South Wales *(see p.10)*, the Museum of Sydney *(see p.6)* or the Australian Museum *(see p.7)*. For rock art, visit the Red Hands Cave in the Blue Mountains National Park *(see p.59)*, or Ku-ring-gai Chase National Park (❹, *see p.59*). NSW National Parks & Wildlife Services, *www.nationalparks.nsw.gov.au*

Sydney, T: 9220 0400,
www.sydney.catholic.org.au

Sydney Aquarium and Sydney Wildlife World ❸

Some 11,500 all-Australian aquatic species call the aquarium home. You can see sharks, giant stingrays, sea turtles, penguins…the list goes on. Check out the largest Great Barrier Reef display in the world, and the all-natural seal habitat. There is even an underwater shark-viewing walkway. Entry isn't cheap but it is worth it. Sydney Wildlife World houses around 6,000 animals in nine quintessential Australian habitats from rainforest to outback. Take the ferry from Circular Quay (see p.6) – it drops you off right outside. *Adm. Open 9am-10pm daily. Aquarium Pier, Darling Harbour, T: 8251 7800, www.sydneyaquarium.com.au, www.sydneywildlifeworld.com.au*

Sydney Fish Market ❷ 5B

Sydney Fish Market is an authentic fishermen's market, the largest in the southern hemisphere. Comprising a working fishing port, wholesale market and fresh food retail market, it showcases a hundred or so species of seafood each day. Aquatic specimens arrive daily at 3pm and are auctioned off from 5.30am the next morning. Take a Behind the Scenes Auction Tour and watch the selling action every Thursday morning at 7am. Choose your lunch from the range of fresh fish, or try your hand at cooking at the Seafood School (*T: 9004 1111*). *Adm. Open from 7am daily. Bank St, Pyrmont, T: 9004 1100, www.sydneyfishmarket.com.au*

Sydney Tower ❷ 5E

For 360-degree views of Sydney from the Blue Mountains (*see p.59*) to the Pacific Ocean, head to Australia's tallest building. At 305 m (1,000 ft), Sydney Tower boasts the southern hemisphere's highest observation deck. The Skywalk is Sydney Tower's newest attraction; you're attached to a safety harness before stepping outdoors to take in the views from a height of 268 m (879 ft). **Tower**: *Adm. Open 9am-10.30pm Sun-Fri, 9am-11.30pm Sat. 100 Market St, Sydney, T: 9333 9222, www.sydneytower.com.au*

The grand façade of Queen Victoria Building

Sealife at the Sydney Aquarium

The Sydney Tower looms tall

Skywalk: *Adm. No bookings required. Open 9.30am-8pm daily. Podium Level, 100 Market St, Sydney, T: 9333 9222, www.skywalk.com.au*

Domain & Botanics

Art Gallery of New South Wales ❷ 4F

An imposing Romanesque exterior gives way to a light-filled, modern space that is renowned for its collections of Australian, Asian, European and contemporary art, and the Yiribana Aboriginal and Torres Strait Islander works. Try the Sunday concerts or the popular Art After Hours (*5pm-9pm Wed*). Keep an eye out for the annual summer blockbuster exhibition.
Open 10am-5pm daily. Art Gallery Rd, The Domain, T: 1800 679 278, www.artgallery.nsw.gov.au

Government House ❷ 2F

Built by English architect Edward Blore between 1837 and 1845 for Governor Macquarie, subsequent New South Wales governors lived here until as recently as 1996. The only way you can explore this romantic Gothic-style mock castle is by guided tour; they're free and depart every half an hour.
House: *Open 10am-3pm Fri-Sun.*
Grounds: *Open 10am-4pm daily. Macquarie St, Sydney, T: 9931 5222, www.hht.net.au/museums/gh/government_house*

Royal Botanic Gardens ❷ 3F

Palm trees, duck ponds and its harbourside location make this Sydney's most beautiful park. The land was cultivated just after the First Fleet arrived (*see box, p.13*), but Governor Phillip set it aside in 1788 when it proved unyielding. In 1816

Entrance to Art Gallery of New South Wales

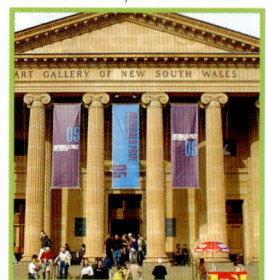

it became the first botanic gardens thanks to Governor Macquarie, and his wife proposed to incorporate a coastal road around what is now Mrs Macquarie's Point (❷ 2G). You can take a free guided tour with one of its volunteers (*T: 9231 8134*). At sunset, look out for the enormous resident fruit bats. *Open 24 hrs. Mrs Macquarie's Rd, Sydney, T: 9231 8111, www.rbgsyd.nsw.gov.au*

The Domain ❷ 4F-5F
A large park stretching from the Art Gallery of New South Wales (*see p.10*) to Macquarie Street, The Domain is predominantly a venue for outdoor concerts. Given its proximity to the city centre and picture-postcard views of the Opera House and Harbour Bridge, The Domain is a popular spot for a short walk or a picnic. It has also played host to outdoor 'free speech' since 1878, following England's lead when it legalised free speech in Hyde Park. Every January it also serves as a principal outdoor concert venue during the Sydney Festival (*www.sydneyfestival.org.au*).

Kings Cross & Surrounds

In the early 19th century, the well-to-do built their homes here in view of the ocean; in the 1920s, it was a meeting place for bohemians, artists and writers. These days it is Australia's most densely populated area and Darlinghurst Road (❷ 6G-7G) is home to bars, strip clubs and hostels. A word of warning: drug addicts frequent the wall at the southern end of Victoria Street so it is an area best avoided.

Elizabeth Bay House ❷ 5H
Overlooking Sydney Harbour from the quietly luxurious Elizabeth Bay, this house was built between 1835 and 1839. John Verge, the most fashionable architect of the day, designed it for colonial secretary Alexander Macleay. *Adm. Open 10am-4.30pm Mon, Fri, Sat (daily in Jan). 7 Onslow Ave, Elizabeth Bay, T: 9356 3022, www.hht.net.au/museums/elizabeth_bay_house*

Lush greenery at the Royal Botanic Gardens

Oxford Street ❷ 6F-7H
A shopping mecca (*see p.18*) and bar heaven, Oxford Street is particularly well known for its variety of gay bars and for the annual Gay and Lesbian Mardi Gras (*see p.60*).

North

Cadman's Cottage ❷ 2E
Built by Francis Greenway in 1816 as the Coxswain's Barracks, Cadman's Cottage is the only remaining testament to early settlement life. The NSW National Parks & Wildlife Service now uses it as their Sydney Harbour National Park Information

Centre (see p.55), from which they run various tours of heritage sites such as Fort Denison and Quarantine Station (below). Open 10am-4.30pm daily. 110 George St, The Rocks (centre entrance George St side), T: 1300 361 967.

Quarantine Station and North Head ❶ 2F

From the Quarantine Station it is well worth the short drive to North Head with its memorable views across the harbour entrance and back towards the city, especially at sunset. From 1832, Quarantine Station protected Sydney's

Koala at Taronga Zoo

residents against epidemics. If there was disease on board an incoming ship, its passengers were isolated here. The station closed in 1984, but you can still tour the burial grounds, shower blocks, disinfecting rooms, hospital and isolation wards. On the frightening night-time Ghost Tour, you'll visit in the dark by torchlight. Other tours available. *North Head Scenic Dr, Manly, T: 9976 6220, www.qstation.com.au*

Sydney Observatory ❷ 2D

Designed by Alexander Dawson in 1858, this is one of Australia's oldest observatories. The sandstone building shields an historic 29-cm (11-inch) lens telescope dating from 1874, a computer-controlled 42-cm (16-inch) telescope, a hydrogen-alpha solar telescope, a 3-D Space Theatre and is surrounded by beautiful gardens. *Book ahead. Open 10am-5pm daily, nightly for tours (must be pre-booked). Watson Rd, Observatory Hill, The Rocks, T: 9921 3485, www.sydneyobservatory.com.au*

Taronga Zoo ❶ 3D

The zoo opened on 7 October 1916 and since then its population has risen to more than 2,000 animals. You can have your picture taken with a koala, attend daily keeper talks and animal shows (don't miss

Sydney for Kids

Sydney Harbour Foreshore Authority organises superb educational tours (T: 9240 8500, www.shfa.nsw.gov.au) of Darling Harbour (see p.7) and The Rocks (see right). The Botanical Gardens wild flying fox (bat) colony is always a fine option for kids, while Taronga Zoo (see above), Sydney Aquarium and Sydney Wildlife World (see p.9) all offer a plethora of captive species, including the ubiquitous natives the roo, croc and koala. Head off to The Entertainment Quarter at Moore Park (❶ 5E) for movie magic (see p.29).

the bird show), tread easy-to-follow trails and catch twilight concerts in summer. A recent addition to the zoo is a multi-million-dollar elephant exhibit. The Sky Safari ride provides a glimpse of the zoo's harbour views. *Adm. Open 9am-5pm daily. Bradleys Head Rd, Mosman, T: 9969 2777, www.zoo.nsw.gov.au*

The Rocks ❷ 2E

In January 1788 the first British convicts set up tents on this once-rocky outcrop. They quickly built dockyards, wharves and warehouses beside timber-framed houses, all tracing the cove's natural ledges. Early residents described the area as being 'on the rocks', and the name stuck. Construction of the Sydney Harbour Bridge (*see p.4*) involved flattening part of the area in the 1930s, but luckily public intervention spared the remainder from a similar fate in the 1970s. *www.therocks.com*

Vaucluse House ❶ 3E

This Gothic-style mansion belonged to William Charles Wentworth, explorer, barrister, patriot and father of the Australian Constitution. The house contains original lavish furnishings. You'll also see stables, a laundry and lovely pleasure gardens. *Adm. Open 9.30am-4pm Fri-Sun Feb-Dec, 9.30am-4pm daily Jan. Wentworth Rd, Vaucluse, T: 9388 7922, www.hht.net.au/museums/vaucluse_house*

The First Fleet

On 13 May 1787, 11 ships left Portsmouth, England, under Captain Arthur Phillip's command. This 'first fleet' was transporting 780 convicts from Britain's overcrowded prisons to Botany Bay ❹, where they would establish Australia's first European colony. Botany Bay didn't appeal to Captain Phillip, so he headed north to Port Jackson and anchored in Sydney Cove (❷ 2E) on 26 January 1788.

The Rocks – saved from demolition

Watsons Bay & Vaucluse ❶ 3E-3F

Watsons Bay and Vaucluse are near Sydney's South Head. Established in 1788, Watsons Bay is Australia's oldest fishing village. Take the ferry there from Circular Quay (*see p.6*) for some delicious fresh fish and chips and soak up the sunshine at the tiny-but-lovely Camp Cove. Explore South Head's natural beauty and shipwreck history with the NSW National Parks & Wildlife Service tours (*see box, p.8*), and admire the dramatic ocean views from the Gap.

Inspiring skyline of Sydney Harbour with the Sydney Opera House at the helm.

sydney places to shop

Though not as renowned for its shopping as for its bridge and beaches, Sydney has a lot to offer fans of the odd spree. Whether you're after antiques, art, books, bikinis or the latest bit of fabric whipped up by the growing number of hip local designers, you'll find it's all well made and well priced. Shops tend to be open on weekdays and Saturdays until 6pm and on Sundays for a shorter period, if at all. Thursday is the night for nocturnal spenders, when shops stay open until 9pm.

buy it places to shop

buy it

Interior of the Queen Victoria Building

Areas

Little clusters of shops are dotted all over Sydney. Some of the stores in this chapter have outlets in the areas listed, where there are also additional shops to look out for.

Central Business District ❷ 4E-5E

The city is jam-packed with major Australian retailers and international labels. The Queen Victoria Building (❷ 5D, *see p.8*) has more than 200 stores and eateries under one 19th-century roof. Pitt Street Mall (❷ 4E-5E) is a patch chock-a-block with stores, malls like the Strand Arcade (❷ 5E) and lots of buskers.
Revenge (Shop 29, T: 9264 4400) Streetwise ladies' fashion.
Woosh (Shop 20, T: 9266 0974) for cutting-edge street-wear for the 25-45s.

Chinatown ❸

Market City (❷ 7D), 9-13 Hay St, Haymarket, T: 9288 8900, www.marketcity.com.au, a huge shopping centre, is home to cheap and cheerful clothing and knick-knack stores and is in the heart of Chinatown (*see p.6*). Independent stores stocking similarly gaudy items pop up all over the area.

Darlinghurst & Paddington ❷ 6E-6F & ❷ 6H-7H

Oxford Street (❷ 6F-7H) is the famous Sydney shopping street. Around it in the Paddington area and on Queen Street (❷ 5D, *see box, p.20*) and Crown Street (❷ 7F) there are plenty more treasure troves to be hunted down.

Oxford Street:
House of Priscilla (*No. 47, T: 9286 3023*) for unique boutique based on the popular Australian film.
Napoleon Perdis (*No. 74, T: 9331 1702*) for professional-quality make-up and stellar makeovers.
Scanlan & Theodore (*No. 122, T: 9380 9388*) for stylish wisps designed locally.

Crown Street:
Route 66 (*255-257, T: 9331 6686*) for cowboy-style clothes, tees and

Oxford Street

jeans. **Wheels & Dollbaby** *(259, T: 9361 3256)* for Agent Provocateur-style (and priced!) clothes 'to snare a millionaire'.

Double Bay ❶ 4E-5E

This quiet, affluent suburb has a few restaurants and stores, all upmarket.
Gary Castles *(45a Bay St, T: 9327 5077)* for shoes.
George *(see p.22) (9 Knox St, T: 9327 1788)* for womenswear and accessories.

Art

2 Danks Street ❶ 5D

Number two's clean white spaces encompass café Danks Street Depot and nine galleries. These include the Gow Langsford Gallery, which exhibits a range of contemporary Australasian artists *(T: 9699 1279)*; Multiple Box *(T: 9690 0213)*, which parades prints, photographs, multiples and new media by international and Australian contemporary artists; the Brenda May Gallery *(T: 9318 1122)*, showcasing two- and three-dimensional Australian artworks, plus a range of one-off jewellery pieces. Meander further along Danks Street for galleries such as Aboriginal Gallery Gondwana *(T: 8399 3492)* on the opposite side of the road.
2 Danks St, Waterloo.

Beach & Surfwear

Bikini Island ❶ 5F

Bondi's beachwear specialist for more than 40 years, every Australian swimwear designer's itsy-bitsy teenie-weenies are here; JETS, Tigerlily, Seafolly, Wahine, Hallican Boodie to up-and-coming brands such as Nookie and Bondeye. The tiny store gets crowded with beachgoers in summer making their annual pilgrimage before hitting the surf. Travellers from the northern hemisphere can take advantage of the special deals during Australia's winter. *38 Campbell Pde, Bondi, T: 9300 9446, www.bikiniisland.com.au*

Mambo ❶ 6C

For Australian-designed, brightly coloured surf- and street-wear for men, women and children, look no further. Started by Dare Jennings in 1984 with the intention of conveying a love of Australia, art, music and life, all with a touch of tongue-in-

Bare all at Bikini Island

Mambo for surf- and street-wear

cheek humour, Mambo has worked with artists such as Australia's Reg Mombassa and Robert Moore, and Japan's Rockin' Jelly Bean as well as Tomo Gokita. They also exhibited at the Art Gallery of NSW (see p.10).
Shop 80, The Corso, Manly, T: 9977 9171, www.mambo.com.au

Books

Berkelouw Books ❶ 6B, ❷ 7G
The Berkelouw family began selling books in Holland in 1812 and their collection has since grown to 800,000 new, rare and antiquarian titles. Browse the selection or sip a coffee at the vibrant on-site café.
Open 9.30am-12midnight daily. 19 Oxford St, Paddington, T: 9360 3200.
Branch: *70 Norton St, Leichhardt, T: 9560 3200, www.berkelouw.com.au*

Gertrude & Alice ❶ 4F
Browse the secondhand selection in this warm, rosy bookstore, then pore over your purchases while grabbing a bite at the café. Bring in your used books too; the store buys as well as sells. There are live music sessions on Wednesday evenings. *46 Hall St, Bondi Beach, T: 9130 5155, www.gertrudeandalice.co.au.*

gleebooks ❷ 7B
This much-loved independent bookstore, which has won Australian Bookstore of the Year four times, is a cache rich with books on the humanities (their speciality), literature and those rare titles often unavailable elsewhere. Down the road at number 191 is gleebooks' Antiquarian, Music & Secondhand and its specialist Children's Bookshop which has, among others, a range of indigenous Australian books for little ones. *49 Glebe Point Rd, Glebe, T: 9660 2333 & 191 Glebe Point Rd, Glebe, T: 9550 5256, www.gleebooks.com.au*

Clothing

Local Designers

Collette Dinnigan ❶ 5E
Collette Dinnigan started in costume design and has since made a name for herself on the international scene, with celebrities such as Naomi Watts and Charlize Theron sporting her designs. Visit her cosy, upmarket store for lacy slips, 1920s beaded pieces and luxurious lingerie.
33 William St, Paddington, T: 9360 6691, www.collettedinnigan.com

---

Where to Go for What
For beachwear, make a beeline for Bondi's (❶ 5F) Campbell Parade and Gould Street. For boutique fashion, try William Street (❶ 5E), home to Collette Dinnigan (*see left*) and frocks-with-flair designer Leona Edmiston (T: 9331 7033). For pre-loved anything, head to Newtown's King Street (❶ 5C-6C) or Glebe Point Road (❷ 6A-7B). For antiques and art, try Queen Street (❶ 5E), where dealers Rex Irwin (T: 9363 3212) and Libby Edwards (T: 9362 9444) and antique jeweller Anne Schofield (T: 9363 1326) are all located.

Romantic designs at Collette Dinnigan

Morrissey ❶ 5E, ❶ 5E

Classically sleek designs for men and women. Peter Morrissey of former Morrissey Edmiston fame has gone solo to create chic, fashionable pieces. Metro shirts for the men and hip, patterned dresses for the female of the species. *372 Oxford St, Paddington, T: 9380 7422.* **Branch:** *Shop 3059, Bondi Junction, Westfield, T: 9387 1166.*

Zimmermann ❶ 5E, ❶ 5E

Stylish tops, pretty dresses in unique prints and unusual fabrics, and beautifully cut coats. Look out for the Zimmermann sisters' vibrant swimwear range, which comes in a myriad of shades, from mangoes, violets, olives and pinks to classic black. Not too pricey, distinctly wearable and catering to the catwalk-thin or girls with curves. *2-16 Glenmore Rd, Paddington, T: 9357 4700.* **Branch:** *Shop 3048, Westfield Bondi Jctn, T: 9387 5111, www.zimmermannwear.com*

Menswear

Herringbone ❶ 3F, ❷ 5D

Made of the finest cotton and with French seams and cuffs, Herringbone shirts are beautifully tailored for an elegant fit. Classic work shirts and ties are available, along with sophisticated tuxedo and cocktail versions in seasonal styles and fabrics. Buy their fine-stitched creations off the rack or have them custom-made. Ladies aren't forgotten; stores stock women's shirts and bags. *Shop 25G, G/F, Queen Victoria Bldg, George St, Sydney, T: 9266 0500.* **Branch:** *7 Macquarie Pl, T: 9252 8106, www.herringbone.com*

Industrie ❶ 5D, ❶ 6F

Funky, metro, casual daywear at reasonable prices, Industrie's pieces range from jeans and cargo pants to polo shirts and blazers with a twist. **Shop:** *LG/27, QVB, George St, T: 9267 4300.* **Branch:** *406 Oxford St, Darlinghurst, T: 9361 5333, www.industrie.com.au*

Womenswear

Dragstar ❶ 5F, ❷ 6C, ❸ 7G

Designer Celia Morris began peddling her 1970s-inspired wares at

Classic menswear at Herringbone

buy it

Bargains at Birkenhead Point

Birkenhead Point, Drummoyne (T: 9181 3922), is the label-lover's heaven. Many major Australian retailers have outlets here selling seconds and last season's leftovers and you'll find kids' clothes, sportswear, shoes, homeware and men's and women's fashion. Mambo (see p.19), David Jones (see right) and Morrissey (see p.21) all have a presence and you can rest those shopped-out feet over a coffee or a bite at one of many eateries around the area. Get there by ferry from Circular Quay (see p.6), or take a 500-series bus down Victoria Street (❷ 7G).

the Bondi Beach Markets (see p.24) in the 1990s and has achieved a loyal following. There is always something for the bargain hunter with tops in retro prints, dresses in vintage fabrics, and leather bags, as well as a fine range of kidswear and jewellery. *535A King St, Newtown, T: 9550 1243, www.dragstar.com.au*

George ❶ 2B, ❶ 5D

Elegant clothes that won't burn a hole in your wallet are George's speciality. With well-cut trousers, smart dresses and floaty, pretty tops in a myriad of colours, there's something for all ages in here. They stock pretty accessories – bags, jewellery and hairpieces that are perfect for race day. *474 Oxford St, Paddington, T: 9357 1072.* **Branches:** *Shop L133, Chatswood Chase, T: 9410 2633.*

Department Stores & Malls

David Jones ❶ 5E, ❷ 5E

Welsh-born retailer David Jones first introduced Sydney to the department store in 1838. He imported 'buckskins, ginghams and waist-coatings' from London and it quickly became the shopping mecca for the well-to-do. These days 'DJ's' is a cool, marble-floored haven for all your upmarket fashion, cosmetics and homeware needs. And their foodhall is to die for (see p.23). *86-108 Castlereagh St, Sydney, T: 9266 5544.* **Branches:** *65-77 Market St, Sydney, T: 9266 5544; Westfield Shopping Plaza, 500 Oxford St, Bondi Jctn, T: 9619 1111, www.davidjones.com.au*

Myer ❶ 5E, ❷ 5D

Australia's Grace Brothers has been revamped and renamed Myer. Each floor houses goods such as children's clothes and toys, homeware from international labels, men's and women's wear and an unrivalled choice of underwear and swimwear. Myer has 65 stores nationally and an extensive list of stores in Sydney – check the website for details and opening times. *436 George St, Sydney, T: 9238 9111.* **Branch:** *Westfield Shopping Plaza, 500 Oxford St, Bondi Jctn, T: 9300 1100, www.myer.com.au*

Westfield Shopping Plaza ❶ 5E
Huge shopping malls that are like cities themselves. You'll find most major commercial retailers here, plus cinemas, food outlets and the above-mentioned department stores. For more information, check the website.
500 Oxford St, Bondi Junction,
T: 9947 8000, www.westfield.com

Everything you need can be got at Myer

Indigenous Products

Boomalli Aboriginal Artists' Cooperative ❶ 6B
A 100-per-cent Aboriginal-owned cooperative that mainly supports indigenous artists from New South Wales but represents other indigenous artists from across Australia. Chock-full of items made by these artists, including books, CDs, cards, posters, publications, glassware and jewellery. There is also an art gallery on site.
55-59 Flood St, Leichhardt,
T: 9560 2541, www.boomalli.org.au

Food, Wine & Cookery

Accoutrement ❶ 2D
A hotchpotch of five shops rolled into one, Accoutrement sells ceramics by the likes of celebrity chef Donna Hay, cooking utensils tried and tested by owner and chef Sue, food, books and cooking lessons. Top Aussie chefs such as Peter Evans of the Hugos Group Restaurants, Bathers' Pavilion's Serge Dansereau (*see p.43*) and Jacqueline Bourke from Sean's Panaroma (*see p.40*) host the classes, in which you can watch the chefs in action, sample their delicious creations and take home the recipes to try on the family. *611 Military Rd, Mosman.*
Shop: *T: 9969 1031.* **Cooking school:** *T: 9969 4911,*
www.accoutrement.com.au

David Jones Foodhall ❶ 5E, ❷ 5E
For anything and everything you could possibly want to gorge on.

Fine wines at David Jones

Every aisle is another feast of pastry swirls, inventive fresh pastas, kosher pickings, cheeses, meats and seafood. An extensive wine selection is a good accompaniment to samples of Sydney's famous rock oysters – plain or served with a dollop of one of their delectable sauces. 'DJ's' can also mix it all up in a hamper given 48 hours' notice. *65-77 Market St, T: 9266 5544.* **Branch:** *Westfield Shopping Plaza, 500 Oxford St, Bondi Junction, T: 9619 1111, www.davidjones.com.au*

Jewellery & Gems

Dinosaur Designs ❶ 5D, ❷ 4E
Funky, chunky jewellery made of a smooth resin – each piece is hand crafted and unique. The bracelets, earrings and necklaces look almost edible, coming in every conceivable shade, from sea-blue and mint to blood orange and chocolate. You can also pick up matching homeware such as vases, bowls and salad servers – all dishwasherproof. *Shop 77, 1/F Strand Arcade, Sydney, T: 9223 2953.* **Branch:** *339 Oxford St, Paddington, T: 9361 3776, www.dinosaurdesigns.com.au*

Opal Fields ❷ 3E
The opal, that lovely, shimmering swirl of blues, pinks, yellows and greens, is Australia's national stone and this store stocks it in all shapes and forms. There are lots of unset opals, as well as jewellery created by ten modern Australian designers. There is also an exhibit of opalised fossils. *190 George St, Sydney, T: 9247 6800, www.opalfields.com.au*

Markets

Sydney has numerous markets where you can find just about anything. The few listed below are worth a

Handmade jewellery at Dinosaur Designs

look for the colours and crowds if nothing else. Take a ferry to Balmain Markets (❶ *4C, every Sat 8.30am-4pm, T: 0418 765 736*) and Rozelle Markets (❶ *5C, every weekend, T: 9818 5373*) or the Tarpeian Market near the Opera House (❷ *2F, Sun, T: 9315 7011*) for Australian arts and crafts. Only cash is accepted.

Bondi Beach Markets ❶ 4F
Located at north Bondi's public school, these bustling markets overflow with knick-knacks and clothes. Vintage dresses, bags and shoes rub shoulders with the creations of young designers testing boundaries with their unique items. If it's raining, abort mission – Bondi ain't the place to be in the wet. *Open 9am-5pm Sun. Bondi Beach Public School (off Campbell Pde), T: 9315 8988.*

Glebe Markets ❷ 7A
For alternative fare, boho-chic, vintage threads, incense, live music and Sydney's best selection of cheap sunglasses as well as new stuff. *Open 7am-4pm Sat.*

Be dazzled at Opal Fields

Glebe Public Sch, 10 Glebe Pt Rd, Glebe, T: 0419 291 449.

Paddington Markets ❶ 5D
These markets have grown to 270 stalls and are now commercial and expensive. But there's a good choice and the quality's decent. *Open 10am-5pm Sat. 395 Oxford St (next to Paddington Uniting Church), Paddington, T: 9331 2923, www.paddingtonmarkets.com.au*

The Rocks Market ❷ 2E
The Rocks Market sells souvenirs by the dozen, and you would be forgiven for thinking it's simply a tourist trap. However, it's worth the detour as designer homeware, arts and craft, cute sticker stalls and baby gumnut fairies for the little 'uns are all on show here – and actually the souvenirs are not too tacky. *Open 10am-5pm Sat & Sun. George St (top of, cnr Playfair St), The Rocks, T: 9240 8717.*

Souvenirs

Outback Centre ❸
Plenty of true blue Aussie knick-knacks to choose from, including a considerable collection of indigenous pieces. If it's art you're after, pop in to the centre's gallery

Browse the many stalls at Paddington Market

out back for regionally sourced work and the theatre for a free Aboriginal show. *28 Darling Walk, 1-25 Harbour St, Darling Hbr, T: 9283 7477, www.outbackcentre.com.au*

GST for Travellers
GST is a 10 per cent tax on all goods and services except those considered essential and is included in listed prices. Travellers leaving Australia can claim a refund on purchases totalling more than A$300 in any one store, provided they were made in the last 30 days and are supported by the goods and receipts. There are facilities for the Tourist Refund Scheme (TRS) at Sydney Airport (*see p.48*) and at cruise-liner terminals. Some stores sell products tax-free (Downtown Duty Free, T: 9233 3166); bring photocopies of your passport and ticket with you.

sydney entertainment

Host to the 2000 Olympic Games and the 2003 Rugby World Cup, Sydney has earned a reputation as a top sporting destination. This laid-back city may be renowned for its outdoor activities and fabulous scenery, but it also has a burgeoning arts scene that just keeps getting better, and whether you're a fan of drama, dance or the movies, you'll be spoilt for choice. Check out some of the smaller theatres and live music venues, as they tend to have more soul than their big sisters. Club-wise, Sydney has finally come out of its shell, and there's no end to the number of hip venues sprouting up all over town. Metro in Friday's Sydney Morning Herald (*see p.61*) always has a detailed list of what's on.

watch it entertainment

Casinos

Star City ❷ 4B
New South Wales' only casino has a TAB lounge (the New South Wales betting service for horse races and sports), sportsbar Star Keno, 200 gaming rooms and panoramic views of Sydney's skyline. *Open 24 hours daily. 80 Pyrmont St, Pyrmont, T: 9777 9000, www.starcity.com.au*

Comedy

The Comedy Store ❶ 5E
Great comedy in a surprisingly intimate setting given its 300 seats. Spots at the licensed bar fill up quickly so get there early to sip on a pricey pre-show tipple. Show your ticket on the night of your show at the Fringe Bar and you'll get 20 per cent off your meal. *Book ahead for popular acts. Shows 8.30pm Tue-Sat nights. 207/122 Lang Rd, The Entertainment Quarter, Moore Pk, T: 9357 1419/ 1300 369 849, www.comedystore.com.au*

Clubs

Free weekly publications *Drum Media* (www.drummedia.com.au) and *3-D World* (www.threedworld.com.au) (*see p.61 for both*) will tell you who's playing where. They're available in newsagents, cafés and music stores.

ARQ ❷ 7F
Encompassing a club and restaurant and wine, oyster and cocktail bars, this is a hotspot for gay and straight clubbers alike, particularly at its Sunday School night. Other regulars include dragshows, the infamous 'foam parties' and 'Fabulon' drag shows (Thu, Sat). *Thu-Sun. 16 Flinders St, Darlinghurst, T: 9380 8700, www.arqsydney.com.au*

Home ❷ 5D
This is no small, backstreet affair, with a recent expansion making it one of the largest club venues in the city. Over 2,000 can be accommodated and an extensive range of music is on offer, including live bands and the latest, internationally renowned DJs. *101 Cockle Bay Wharf, Darling Harbour, T: 9266 0600, www.homesydney.com*

Tank Nightclub

Tank Nightclub ❷ 3E
Tank's been around the traps for a while and still maintains a loyal following. Once a part of the Tank Stream, which supplied early Sydney's water, the building retains much of the original structure. God is a DJ playing house music, and compliance with the 'funky club wear to smart-casual' dress code is essential. *3 Bridge Ln, Sydney, T: 9240 3000, www.tankclub.com.au*

Cinemas

Sydney has countless cinemas. For mainstream cinema listings check the newspapers or *Metro* (*see p.61 for all*), which has more extensive schedules. Many cinemas have a free seating policy.

Arthouse

Dendy Cinemas ❶ 6C
A chain of arthouse cinemas with two locations in Sydney, Dendy allegedly records the highest per screen averages of 'quality cinema' in town. At Dendy Opera Quays, seniors can enjoy cheap tickets and free morning tea at the day's first session on Wednesdays and Thursdays. Both cinemas have a Monday discount. **Dendy Opera Quay:** *2 E Circular Quay, Circular Quay, T: 9247 3800.* **Branch:** *261-263 King St, Newtown, T: 9550 5699, www.dendy.com.au*

Govinda's & Movie Room ❷ 6G
A cheap and cheerful place to grab a tasty vegetarian Indian meal and catch a film seated on cushions or one of the sofas – here you're even encouraged to take your shoes off. Try the dinner-and-show package. *112 Darlinghurst Rd, Darlinghurst, T: 9380 5155, www.govindas.com.au*

The Orpheum ❶ 3D
Enjoy a traditional cinema experience in this restored 1935 six-cinema complex. The Art-Deco fittings and ambience include a piano bar and original working Wurlitzer pipe organ. *380 Military Rd, Cremorne, T: 9908 4344, www.orpheum.com.au*

Blockbusters

Hoyts ❶ 5E
Mainly showing blockbusters, this is a major venue in the Moore Park Entertainment Quarter, where you can plump for its La Première service for a higher price and enjoy first-class seats, food and wine. For arthouse films, Hoyts Cinema Paris (T: 9332 1633) is further along Bent St. *Bent St, The Entertainment Quarter, Moore Pk, T: 1900 9 HOYTS, www.hoyts.com.au*

Imax

IMAX Theatre ❸
Ten times larger than normal, this is the world's largest movie screen. Films, in 3-D and 2-D, are usually documentaries on topics such as the ocean, sharks, outer space, or even the human body, which look amazing on a massive screen. *Showings every hour, on the hour. Open 10am-10pm daily. 31 Wheat Rd, Darling Hbr, T: 9281 3300, www.imax.com.au*

Sydney's IMAX Theatre

Sydney Opera House

This world-famous venue (*see p.5*) hosts a vast range of productions and several seasonal regulars.

watch it

watch it

The Australian Ballet (see p.31) performs March to May and November to December, and the Australian Chamber Orchestra (www.aco.com.au) between February and November. Opera Australia (www.opera-australia.org.au) is a series of operas performed through both the winter (June to November) and summer (January to March) seasons. Sydney Theatre Company (www.sydneytheatre.com) shows plays year-round at the Drama Theatre (see right). Call direct for bookings or ask about their performance packages. *Bennelong Pt, Sydney, T: 9250 7777, www.sydneyoperahouse.com*

The following venues are all housed under the Sydney Opera House's roof.

Concert Hall ❷ 2F
The high-vaulted ceilings cater to acoustic performances and the 18 acrylic rings hanging from the ceiling enhance sound by reflecting it back to the orchestra. Though the Sydney Symphony (www.symphony.com) dominates, it's also used for jazz, chamber, folk and popular music. Capacity is 2,679.

Drama Theatre ❷ 2F
Featuring an extensive programme of contemporary performances of song and dance, there are all-round good sightlines thanks to the raked seats. Both the Sydney Theatre Company (see left) and the Bell Shakespeare Company (www.bellshakespeare.com.au) perform here. Capacity is 544.

Opera Theatre ❷ 2F
Opera Australia (www.opera-australia.org.au) and The Australian Ballet (see p.31) are the main presenters in this proscenium-arch lyric theatre. Some seats have restricted sightlines. Capacity is 1,507.

Playhouse ❷ 2F
A fully raked auditorium offers good views from every seat. Sydney Opera House, the Sydney Theatre and Bell Shakespeare companies (see left) stage productions here. Capacity is 398.

The Studio ❷ 2F
The most intimate venue in the Opera House is used for musical and contemporary performances. Capacity is 318 – at a pinch.

Dance & Theatre

Sydney's theatre and dance culture is diverse and thriving; there are many venues to choose from depending on what you want to see, be it a musical, play, ballet performance or a rock gig.

Sydney Opera House at night

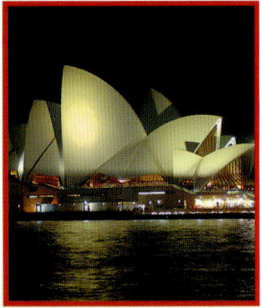

Classical Music

City Recital Hall ❷ 4D
An intimate chamber music hall with a rectangular auditorium and two balconies encircling the stage. Specifically catering to music performances, it's designed to enhance sound quality. *Angel Pl, T: 8256 2222, www.cityrecitalhall.com*

Contemporary ballet by Sydney Dance Company

Dance

The Australian Ballet
Founded in 1962 and with a troupe consisting of more than 70 dancers, The Australian Ballet performs around 200 contemporary and traditional classical works annually. Melbourne is its home town, but it also regularly appears in Sydney. *Lvl 3, 10 Hickson Rd, The Rocks. T: 1300 369 741, www.australianballet.com.au*

Sydney Dance Company ❷ 1D
Australia's premier contemporary dance company's troupe is renowned for its technical finesse and artistry, showcasing at least one new original work per year, often with scores by Australian composers. It performs in Sydney and also tours nationally and across Europe, Asia, North and South America. *Pier 4, Hickson Rd, Walsh Bay, T: 9221 4811, www.sydneydancecompany.com*

Drama

Belvoir St Theatre ❶ 5D
When the Nimrod Theatre faced demolition, Sue Hill and Chris Westwood convinced friends in the arts, including actors Sam Neill and Nicole Kidman, to chip in towards an innovative new space. *25 Belvoir St, Surry Hills, T: 9699 3444, www.belvoir.com.au*

Old Fitzroy Theatre at The Old Fitzroy Hotel ❷ 5G
Edgy performances by Australia's up-and-coming actors accompanied by tasty laksa at the shabby pub next door; try the Old Fitz special, 'Beer, Laksa and Show'. *129 Dowling St, Woolloomooloo. T: 9294 4296, www.oldfitzroy.com.au*

Wharf Theatre ❷ 1D
The Sydney Theatre Company is the country's premier theatre company and maintains its lovely waterside base on the site of the old Bond Stores. The annual calendar features five home-grown pieces, along with traditional and controversial international works. Pop to the harbourside bar for a pre-show drink. *Pier 4/5, Hickson Rd, Walsh Bay, T: 9250 1777, www.sydneytheatre.com.au*

Ticketing Tips

For theatre, musical and sports tickets, try Ticketek (*T: 132 849, www.ticketek.com.au*) and Ticketmaster7 (*T: 1300 136 166, www.ticketmaster7.com*). Moshtix (*T: 9209 4614, www.moshtix.com.au*) is the source for many live music tickets.

Musicals

Capitol Theatre ❷ 7D

On the site of a marketplace that was once home to a circus, playhouse and sideshows, the building took its current form in 1927. The beautifully restored structure, where you can catch a musical, play or dance performance, is full of old-world charm.
*13 Campbell St, Haymarket,
T: 9320 5000,
www.capitoltheatre.com.au*

Lyric Theatre ❷ 4B

Hailed as Australia's best commercial venue for performances such as musicals, ballet, theatre and opera, and boasting an enormous stage and orchestra pit. *T: 1300 658 009* about show packages. *Star City, 80 Pyrmont St, Pyrmont, T: 9657 8500,
www.starcity.com.au*

Theatre Royal ❷ 4E

This 1,133-seat venue predominantly hosts mainstream musicals. It has the steepest seats in Sydney, so watch out if you've got long legs or suffer from vertigo! *108 King St, MLC Centre, Sydney, T: 1300 795 012.*

The Capitol Theatre dates from 1927

Jazz Venues

Wine Banq ❷ 4E

An intimate basement wine bar earning a loyal following for convivial jazz sessions and gigs with occasional well knowns like Harry Connick Jnr. *53 Martin Pl, Sydney, T: 9222 1919,
www.winebanq.com.au*

The Basement ❷ 3E

A perfect dingy jazz venue. Come early for an uninterrupted view or reserve a table at the front for one of their dinner-and-show deals. When livelier acts play, out go the tables and in comes the dance floor. *29 Reiby Pl, Circular Quay,
T: 9251 2797,
www.thebasement.com.au*

Rock & Pop Venues

Hordern Pavilion ❶ 5E

Originally built in 1924, this heritage-listed venue has seen its share of international performers, such as Frank Sinatra, Coldplay and

Nick Cave & the Bad Seeds, all of whom have graced its stage. In the 1980s, it was here that Australia's rave scene was born. *Cnr Lang Rd & ANZAC Pde, The Entertainment Quarter, Moore Pk, T: 9921 5333, www.hordernpavilion.com.au*

Metro Theatre ❷ 6D, ❸

A standing-only venue showcasing new and established bands and DJs. *624 George St, Sydney, T: 9550 3666, www.metrotheatre.com.au*

Sydney Entertainment Centre ❸

Seats 12,000, so major acts tend to play here but it's a bit soulless. *35 Harbour St, Darling Hbr,*

Live music at The Basement

T: 9320 4200, www.sydentcent.com.au

Participation Sport

Sydney is a city that absolutely loves outdoor pursuits, so it's not surprising that there is such a wide range of sporting events and activities available here. Purchase event tickets through Ticketek (*see box, p.32*).

Biking

Bicentennial Park Information Centre Bike Hire ❻

Choose from the 8-km (5-mile) Olympic, 15-km (9-mile) River Heritage and 6-km (4-mile) Parklands Circuits. Ask at the centre for a map. **Park:** Cycle hire is available from Centennial Park Cycles, which operate stands in Centennial Park and Bicentennial Park or at their shop in Randwick (*50 Clovelly Rd, T: 9398 5027, www.cyclehire.com.au*). *Australia Ave, Sydney Olympic Pk, T: 9714 7888.*

Diving

Pro Dive ❶ 6F

Catering for all levels of experience, Pro Dive provides good-quality services and all equipment for scuba-diving. *27 Alfreda St, Coogee, T: 1800 820 820, www.prodive.com.au*

Golf

Sydney has a plethora of courses from international standard to pitch and putt. The visitor should try one of the many seaside courses with its sublime aesthetics. These include *Mona Vale, North Shore* ❹*, T: 9999 4266* and *the New South Wales Golf Club, La Perouse* ❹*, T: 9661 1455. A useful website for detail is www.iseekgolf.com/courses*

Gyms

No 1 Martin Place ❷ 4E

Five-star health facilities in the heritage-listed GPO building. *Open 6am-9pm Mon-Thu, 6am-8pm Fri, 8am-6pm Sat & Sun. 4/F, 1 Martin Pl, Sydney, T: 9232 1500, www.no1thehealthclub.com.au*

watch it

Kayaking

Sydney Harbour Kayaks ❶ 2D
A top location offering the opportunity to explore the chaotic Middle Harbour, but also quiet bush-clad tributaries reaching far inland.
Spit Bridge, Mosman, T: 9960 4389, www.sydneyharbourkayaks.com.au

Sailing

Home to the annual Sydney to Hobart race, the city has a large and avid sailing community for which the sparklingly beautiful Sydney Harbour provides the perfect backdrop.

Kids at Let's Go Surfing Surf School

Sydney By Sail
The Sydney Maritime Museum offers its own introductory or instruction courses. *Sydney Maritime Museum, Darling Harbour, T: 9280 1110, www.sydneybysail.com*

Surfing

Let's Go Surfing ❶ 4F
This centre offers beginner, intermediate, advanced and children's in one-on-one or group settings. The package is comprehensive; you'll get all the gear and sunscreen to boot.
128a Ramsgate Ave, Bondi Beach, T: 9365 1800, www.letsgosurfing.com.au

Swimming Pools

Andrew (Boy) Charlton Pool ❷ 3G
Situated on a site known as the Fig Tree, this was once a bathing place for the Aboriginal Eora people and, later, the colonial settlers. Recent renovations have resulted in its becoming one of the most spectacular pools in Sydney, with stunning harbour views. Adm. Open 6am-7pm daily, Oct-Apr. *Mrs Macquarie's Rd, The Domain, T: 9358 6686, www.abcpool.org*

Bondi Icebergs Pool ❶ 5F
So close to the sea it's practically in it, waves often splash dramatically

---

Bangarra Dance Theatre
This group blends 40,000 years' worth of traditional Aboriginal and Torres Strait Islander culture with contemporary indigenous dance and music. Bangarra means 'to make a fire' in the Wiradjeri language of New South Wales and, aiming to give voice to social and political issues, these guys know how to heat things up. The performers use rituals and storytelling, often touring regionally and internationally. Check for Sydney shows. *T: 9251 5333, www.bangarra.com.au*

into its eight lanes. There is also a shallow 20-m (66-ft) pool for children, plus disabled access and changing facilities. *Adm. Closed Thu. 1 Notts Ave, Bondi, T: 9130 4804, www.icebergs.com.au*

Yoga

Ashtanga Yoga Space ❷ 7G

As the name suggests, this school focuses on the Ashtanga practices of 92-year-old Indian teacher Sri K. Pattabhi. Out of towners can join classes without enrolling for lengthy periods. Call or email for details. *The Verona Building, 17 Oxford St, Paddington, T: 9360 7602, www.ashtangayogaspace.com.au*

Spectator Sport

Major Venues

ANZ Stadium ❻

The stadium seats a mammoth 81,500 at Australian Football League games. Tours available. *Edwin Flack Ave, Sydney Olympic Pk, T: 8765 2300, www.anzstadium.com.au*

Aussie Stadium ❶ 5D

Tours of the stadium depart 10am and 1pm, Monday to Friday. Call T: 1300 724 737 for details. *Moore Pk Rd, Paddington, T: 9360 6601, www.aussiestadium.com.au*

Sydney Cricket Ground ❶ 5D

Cricket has been played at the 'SCG', as Sydneysiders have dubbed it, since the 19th century. It is a no-smoking area but booze is available so don't bring your own. *Moore Pk Rd, Paddington, T: 9360 6601, www.sydneycricketground.com.au*

Cricket

Cricket has a huge following in Australia, and Sydney plays host to many of the major cricket series. Games are played at the Sydney Cricket Ground and ANZ Stadium (see left).

Rugby League/Rugby Union/Soccer/AFL

New South Wales and Queensland play Rugby League in the State of Origin. Rugby Union is played in the Trinations matches between Australia, New Zealand and South Africa. League and Union events are played at Aussie Stadium and ANZ Stadium (see left). Australia's reputation on the international soccer scene reached heady new heights with the success of the national team in the 2006 World Cup, when they reached the last 16. The Australian Football League (AFL) was invented in 1857 by Tom Wills to keep cricketers fit during winter. Today 16 teams participate and games take place at ANZ Stadium and the SCG.

Bondi Icebergs Pool

watch it

sydney places to eat and drink

Australia is a country rich in natural produce and Sydney has access to the very best of it. Fruit and vegetables from Queensland, livestock from New South Wales, wines from every state and seafood from Sydney's own coastal waters; this and the city's melting pot of Asian and European cultural backgrounds makes for fresh, tasty and authentic dining experiences. Although locals like to cook for themselves almost as much as they like to eat out, the city's restaurant scene is exciting and thriving, and it's not hard to find good-quality food that is, more often than not, accompanied by a fine view of Sydney's most loved asset: its harbour. It's advisable to book ahead – particularly at the weekends.

taste it places to eat and drink

Price Guide Per Person
Prices are for a three-course meal for one without alcohol, including tax and tip.
$ = under $30
$$ = between $30-50
$$$ = between $50-75
$$$$ = above $75

Atmosphere

Chinta Ria... The Temple of Love
$$ ❶ 5D, ❸
Despite the cheesy name, this circular, dimly lit Malaysian restaurant is a cool hideaway on the roof terrace of Cockle Bay Wharf.

Relax at Chinta Ria

A giant, fat, happy Buddha watches over the friendly staff as they serve dishes that are both tasty and occasionally spicy. *Level 2, The Roof Terrace, Cockle Bay Wharf, Darling Pk, 201 Sussex St, T: 9264 3211, www.chintaria.com*

Brunch

A long and leisurely weekend breakfast that turns into lunch is how the locals like it. Below are two of the best, but Bathers' Pavilion (see p.43), and Hugo's Lounge in Kings Cross (see p.44) also serve a mean brunch if you're not pinching your pennies.

bills $$ ❷ 6G, 7F
bills has long been famous for owner Bill Granger's fluffy ricotta hotcakes with honeycomb butter, sweetcorn fritters with roast tomato, spinach and bacon, and fabulous coffee. It's a cosy room with a communal table and newspapers everywhere. The Surry Hills location, which is open for dinner and is easier to get into, has a slightly colder feel and languid service. *433 Liverpool St, Darlinghurst,*

T: 9360 9631. **Branch:** *359 Crown St, Surry Hills, T: 9360 4762, www.bills.com.au*

Caffe Salina $$ ❶ 5F
Locally popular for breakfast or brunch, especially at the weekend. Good coffee, good value and the perfect spot to absorb the leisurely Bronte buzz. Afterwards take a stroll along the scenic coastal path to Bondi Beach. *Open for breakfast and lunch Mon-Sun, dinner Fri-Sun. 477 Bronte Road, Bronte Beach, T: 02 9369 4012, www.caffesalina.com.au*

Cheap Lunch

I'm Starvin! $ ❷ 3E
Haloumi, artichokes, prosciutto, parmesan and chorizo are just some

Fresh, gourmet fillings at I'm Starvin!

of the fresh fillings that are teamed with huge hunks of bread to create gourmet feasts all washed down with freshly squeezed juices. Takeaway only, so head to Circular Quay (see p.6) to savour your sandwich in the park. *Closed Sat & Sun. Shop 6, 2 Bridge St (cnr George St), Sydney, T: 9247 5377.*

Chinese

East Ocean $$ ❷ 6D
If you can ignore the condemned crayfish and crab in the huge tanks on entry, for sheer variety this is one of the best of Chinatown's rash of restaurants. Seating over 400, so don't expect a quiet romantic dinner but people-watching is all part of the experience. Try the Yum Cha-a speciality. *Open daily for lunch and dinner. 421-426 Sussex St, Haymarket, T: 9212 4198.*

> **Tips on Tipping**
> Tipping in Australia isn't obligatory, but is definitely appreciated. The standard rate is an additional 10 per cent in recognition of good service. In bars and clubs, when you receive your change, it's polite to leave your cent coins for the bartender, though again this is entirely up to you.

Coffee

A love of coffee has led Sydney to perfect the art of making it and the city is peppered with tiny cafés where the coffee is rich and aromatic. Make sure you know your terminology, though. If you're after a café latte, ask for a 'flat white'. If you want an espresso, it's a 'short black' and a black coffee is a 'long black'.

Bar Coluzzi $ ❷ 6G
Red, cluttered walls give this place a shabby charm. Run by Italians, the coffees are superbly aromatic, the panini are deliciously fresh and the Italian pastries soft and filled with a thick buttercup-coloured cream. *Open 5am-7pm daily. 322 Victoria St, Darlinghurst, T: 9380 5420.*

La Buvette $ ❷ 4H
A hole-in-the-wall serving some of Sydney's best coffee, this funky Italian-style café is really busy at the weekends. *35 Challis Ave, Potts Point, T: 9358 5113.*

Greek

Perama $$$ ❶ 6C
Whitewashed walls and simple décor evoke the mood of a Greek holiday. The food – ancient Byzantine, Ottoman and modern influences blended with seasonal Asian produce – would have even Dionysus smiling. Whitebait with ouzo mayonnaise, slow-baked lamb skaras and moussaka with bechamel are all light. Chef David Tsirekas also makes a divine caramel baklava ice cream… Mount Olympus here you come. *Closed Mon. 88 Audley St, Petersham, T: 9569 7534, www.perama.com.au*

Indian

Zaaffran $$ ❷ 5C
A consistent award winner promising authentic cooking 'just as an Indian

mother would make'. With the restaurant quickly earning a reputation as the city's best and a bustling affair, one wonders just how many mothers are involved. Beyond the fine cuisine the harbour and city skyline views are also a memorable feature. *Open daily for lunch and dinner. Level 2, 345 Harbourside Shopping Centre, Darling Harbour, T: 9211 8900, www.zaaffran.com.au*

Italian

Dolcetta Café and Providore $$ ❷ 5G

A small, no-nonsense Italian that enjoys a loyal local following for its fine coffee, social atmosphere and

Dine with Sydney's style set at Otto

great-value, quality cuisine. *Open for breakfast and lunch Sun-Mon, dinner Tue-Fri. Shop 4, 165 Victoria St, Potts Point, T: 9326 9899.*

Otto $$$ ❷ 4G

Sparkling wharf-side views, socialites sporting Louis Vuitton and Jackie O sunglasses and suits closing deals; part-owner and 'King of Radio' John Laws oversees it all. The award-winning cuisine is modern Italian with a focus on seafood. *Closes 9pm on Sun. The Wharf, 6 Cowper Rd, Woolloomooloo, T: 9368 7488, www.otto.net.au*

Japanese

Sushi E $$$ ❷ 3E

Delicious, classic sushi served at a long marble bar. The chefs trained in Japan, so if you're feeling adventurous, let them throw together something special for you. There are other tasty dishes if you are not enthusiastic about sushi. Situated next to Hemmesphere (*see p.44*), it's a little more low-key – but not much. *Closed Sun & Mon. Level 4,*

252 George St, T: 9240 3044, www.merivale.com

Modern Australian

Sean's Panaroma $$$ ❶ 4F

Sean's offers gorgeous feasts focusing on seasonal Australian produce. Dishes such as aubergine soup with cream and oysters, snapper fillet braised in olive oil with artichokes, and white chocolate and rosemary nougat make this a must. If you're after a peaceful meal, be warned, this tiny space amplifies sound. *Closed Mon & Tue. 270 Campbell Pde, Bondi, T: 9365 4924, www.seanspanaroma.com.au*

The Australian Hotel $$ ❷ 2D

Modern Australian can mean many things, but it does not get much more Aussie than the menu list at this iconic pub near The Rocks. How about a kangaroo steak, some crocodile, or even a spot of emu? All of which goes down even better with a cool Aussie beer – or so they say! Arrive early to get a street table. *Open daily for lunch and dinner. 100 Cumberland St, The Rocks, T: 9247 2229, www.australianheritagehotel.com*

Pizza

Hugo's Pizza $$$ ❷ 5H

The pizzas are gourmet and so are the people. Thin dough discs topped with gorgonzola, pork belly or puttanesca are served on wooden slabs to hungry diners reclining on hip, chocolate-coloured, leather couches. *33 Bayswater Rd, Kings Cross, T: 9337 4411, www.hugos.com.au*

La Disfida $ ❶ 5B

This place has the reputation for serving the best pizzas that can be

Get lined up for Japanese Sushi E

found in Sydney. The pizzas here are thin-crusted, with traditional Italian toppings (so no pineapple for all you Hawaiian fans), and the surroundings are equally authentic. Try their signature Barletta variety and arrive early to avoid a long wait. *Closed Mon & Tue. 109 Ramsay St, Haberfield, T: 9798 8299.*

Drinking & Smoking Policies

You can no longer smoke in any enclosed public spaces in Australia. These tightened smoking laws have been countered in Sydney with a relaxation to its licensing laws that now allow patrons to consume alcohol in cafés and restaurants without the accompaniment of food. Some restaurants however don't stock alcohol and you have to 'Bring Your Own' (BYO). This is a good thing since, although you'll be charged a corkage fee, you avoid the mark-up.

Pubs

The Oaks $ ❶ 3D

Sydney has plenty of pubs dishing out hearty meals, but the Oaks is something of a North Shore institution. More like a pub complex than a quaint drinking hole, you can soak up the atmosphere in the courtyard under the great namesake tree and sample full set menus or generous BBQ buffets. *118 Military Rd, Neutral Bay, T: 9953 5515.*

Seafood

Doyles $$$$ ❶ 3E, ❷ 5B

This institution has been around for five generations. Doyles on the Beach, with lovely views across Watsons Bay (*see p.13*), is the oldest, best-known and most expensive. For cheap, fresh oysters and seafood, visit Fisherman's Wharf take-away service and have a picnic.
Doyles on the Beach: *11 Marine Pde, Watsons Bay, T: 9337 2007.*
Doyles Fisherman's Wharf: *Watsons Bay Wharf, T: 9337 6214.*
Doyles at the Sydney Fish Market:

Packed house at Doyles

(see p.9), Bank St, Pyrmont, T: 9337 1350.

Pellegrini's Café $$ ❶ 4B

The water views are stunning from this well-kept Balmain secret, situated on Elliot Street Wharf. It serves gluten-free, modern Australian fare at reasonable prices. The seafood in particular is deliciously fresh, although the beef is occasionally overcooked. *107 Elliot St Wharf, Balmain, T: 9810 4551.*

Special Occasions

Café Sydney $$$$ ❷ 3E

A cool oasis amid the bustle of Circular Quay's mass of buskers and tourists (see p.6). The chefs expertly combine Asian, Mediterranean and Australian flavours and serve them with tipples from extensive wine and killer cocktail lists. Perfect for a lazy Sunday afternoon – the Harbour Bridge (see p.4) is resplendent, the wood-grilled seafood is delicious and live jazz fills the air. Ask to be seated on the balcony. *5th Fl, Customs Hse, 31 Alfred St, Circular Quay, T: 9251 8683, www.cafesydney.com*

Rockpool $$$$ ❷ 3E

Known the world over as the must-do Sydney dining experience, chef Neil Perry has been presenting diners with sumptuously experimental fare in a classically modern grey-and-brown setting for more than 15 years. The wine list features the best that Australia can offer. *107 George St, The Rocks, T: 9252 1888, www.rockpool.com*

Tetsuya's $$$$ ❸

A night at Tetsuya's is a gastronomical adventure in 12 delectable parts. The changing menu features delicately flavoured dishes such as their signature melt-in-the-mouth confit of Tasmanian trout with *conbu* (deep-sea seaweed from north Japan) and the dégustation menu includes a selection of half glasses of wine to complement each course. Arrive with an empty stomach and book well in advance as it is a very popular restaurant. *Closed Sun & Mon. 529 Kent St, Sydney, T: 9267 2900, www.tetsuyas.com*

Fusion flavours at Café Sydney

Thai

Longrain $$$ ❷ 6E
Some might be sceptical about a German-born chef cooking Thai food, but Martin Boetze's creations are bursting with exquisite flavours and perfectly balance sweet, sour and spicy. Set in a large, hundred-year-old warehouse, the idea is to order banquet-style so you can try everything. Don't miss the famous eggnet, a mix of pork and vegetables with a delicate egg covering. *Closed Sun. 85 Commonwealth St, Surry Hills, T: 9280 2888, www.longrain.com*

Sailors Thai $$$ ❷ 2E
The former 1840s 'Sailors' Home' now houses Sailors Thai and its cheaper little sister upstairs. It maintains the original stone walls and has added lime, rose and lemon panelling to create surroundings as lively as the food. The menu combines Australian meats and seafood with succulent Thai flavours. Try the three-course tasting menu. *Closed Sun. 106 George St, The Rocks, T: 9251 2466.*

Vegetarian

Bodhi Restaurant & Bar $$ ❷ 5F
This little restaurant serves vegetarian *yum cha* (dim sum) and other dishes, hidden away in the environs of St Mary's Cathedral. Inside, Buddha statues and wooden benches make it a very Zen spot for a quiet bite away from all the noise of Kings Cross (see p.11). *Cook & Phillip Pk, cnr College and William Sts, Sydney, T: 9360 2523.*

View

Aqua Dining $$$$ ❶ 4D
What was once the North Sydney Olympic Pool caretaker's lodge is now a long, thin restaurant with fantastic harbour views. Suspended above the pool and so close to Luna Park (see p.4) you could touch it, Aqua serves French- and Italian-influenced fare. Save room for chef Jeff Turnbull's delicious desserts, with an emphasis on chocolate, especially at lunchtime. *Cnr Paul St & Northcliff St, Milsons Pt, T: 9964 9998, www.aquadining.com.au*

Bathers' Pavilion Restaurant & Café $$–$$$$ ❶ 2E
With pretty Balmoral Beach as the backdrop, Serge Dansereau melds French, Australian and Asian flavours in this sleek restaurant. The next-door café, with its Moroccan ochre-coloured walls and simple flavours, is the more relaxed hangout for the north's yummy mummies, families and twenty-somethings. Both do a tasty brunch. *4 The Esplanade, Balmoral Beach, T: 9969 5050, www.batherspavilion.com.au*

Icebergs Dining Room & Bar $$$$ ❶ 5F
Perched dramatically over the pools at south Bondi (see p.4), the décor

Great views at the Bathers' Pavilion

here is simple, with whites and greys giving it an airy feel. The clientèle are similarly cool, though not everyone comes here to be seen – many simply make the journey for Roberto Marchetti's modern Mediterranean food. *1 Notts Ave, Bondi, T: 9365 9000, www.idrb.com*

Bars

Hemmesphere ❷ 3E

There's a hush of money in this spacious, upscale, ottoman-filled bar. Make sure you dress the part – and come prepared to act it. An evening here will burn a hole in your wallet, but the delicate bar food and

Discreet, pricey elegance at Hemmesphere

yummy cocktails are well worth it. Sample Northern Lights, an absinthe-based cocktail that will make you see double. *Closed Sun & Mon. 4/F Establishment Hotel, 252 George St, T: 9240 3040, www.merivale.com*

Hugo's Lounge ❷ 6H

Hugo's likes pretty people so there's lots of eye candy at this sophisticated joint. It also means there is a strict door policy. Check out the Sunday night DJ session for half-price Cointreau cocktails – entry A$10 after 8pm. *Closed Mon. Level 1, 33 Bayswater Rd, Kings Cross, T: 9357 4411.*

Manly Wharf Hotel ❶ 1E

Light, open spaces, balconies and a wooden bar on a jetty overlooking the water make this a superb choice for a lazy afternoon beer. A great place to watch the sun go down. The hotel's restaurant also serves gastropub fare. *Manly Wharf, E Esplanade, Manly, T: 9977 1266, www.manlywharfhotel.com.au*

Opera Bar ❷ 2F

Touting itself as having 'the best beer garden in the world' and yet without

Hurry to Harry's ❷ 4G

For six decades, against a pretty Woolloomooloo Wharf backdrop, this little pie cart has been dishing out old-fashioned Aussie pies and peas. Harry (Tiger) Edwards set it up in the 1930s as a late-night beacon to sailors, cabbies, cops and celebrities. The City Council required mobile caravans to move at least 30 cm (12 inches) a day and 'Harry's cart' became 'Harry's Café de Wheels'. After a late-night booze you can get a mean 'Tiger' pie with mushy peas for under A$5. *T: 9357 3074, www.harryscafedewheels.com.au*

a plant pot in sight, there is no denying the spectacular position overlooking Circular Quay, The Rocks, Harbour Bridge (see p.4) and of course the iconic 'sails' of the Opera House (see pp.5-6, 29-30). As such it is a must for visitors to Sydney and late afternoon and early evening is the ideal time for a glass of wine or a cocktail, just as the city skyline lights up. *Lwr Concourse, Sydney Opera Hse, Bennelong Pt, T: 9247 1666, www.operabar.com.au*

Redoak Boutique Beer Café ❷ 4D

The owners brew their own award-winning European-style beers, serving them like fine wines in glasses and with whatever food best complements the flavours. Their signature beer is the Framboise Froment, which is brewed Belgian-style with fresh raspberries. Boutique beer, boutique prices. *Closed Sun. 201 Clarence St, Sydney, T: 9262 3303, www.redoak.com.au*

Sapphire Suite ❷ 5H

An elegant lounge bar filled with dim, sapphire-tinted lights and chocolate-coloured leather booths, Sapphire Suite is a jewel in the sea of cheesy bars in Kings Cross (see p.11). If the music is too loud, you can go downstairs to the quieter 'club' area and sip your cocktail under the sparkling spherical chandeliers. The action starts after 11pm. *Open Fri-Sun 6pm-late. 2 Kellett St, Kings Cross, T: 9331 0058, www.sapphiresuite.com*

The Colombian Hotel ❷ 6F

Particularly popular with gay and lesbian Sydneysiders, watch the Oxford Street (see p.18) set go by from this open, casual, street-level bar. A buzzy spot for a night out or a leisurely Sunday afternoon beer; alternatively sip a cocktail in the cool, quiet bar upstairs. *Open daily 10am-5am. 117-123 Oxford St (cnr Oxford & Crown Sts), Darlinghurst, T: 9360 2151.*

The Lord Nelson ❷ 2D

Established in 1841, it is one of the nation's oldest pubs and a long established favourite on the Rock's 'cosmopolitan' pub-crawl circuit. It retains a congenial, historic feel and

The Opera Bar glowing at night

serves up its own tasty home-brewed beers ranging from the mild to darn right dangerous. If it all gets too much consider the fine accommodation upstairs. *19 Kent St, cnr Argyll, The Rocks, T: 9251 4044.*

Water Bar ❷ 4G

Part of the Blue Sydney hotel, the Water Bar takes advantage of the structure of its heritage-listed wharf home (see p.57); this has low, secluding walls, giving you a full view of the lofty roof. Plush red couches, award-winning cocktails and dim, intimate lighting make this the ideal spot for a bit of budget-blowing fun. *The W Hotel, 6 Cowper Wharf Rd, Woolloomooloo, T: 8356 2575, www.tajhotels.com*

sydney practical information

Sydney is one of the largest cities in the world; including its surrounds, it stretches 80 km (50 miles) from north to south and 70 km (43 miles) east to west. It has an extensive public transport system that spans much of its length and breadth. Sydney's ferries are the most pleasant way to travel, as well as being one of the cheapest, and provide harbour views while you go from A to B; buses and trains are plentiful and on hand to take you anywhere that you wish to go in this sprawling city – and most of its museums and sights are within reach of the Central Business District. A string of well-equipped tourist information centres will help you find your way.

know it practical information

Tourist Information

Sydney Visitor Centre ❷ 2E

Sydney's most helpful resource for tourists, whose multilingual staff can book tours or hotels and arrange cheap transport tickets from their premises (make sure you check the blackboards for the deals of the day). Open 9.30am-5.30pm daily.
Branches: Cnr Playfair and Argyll Sts, The Rocks, T: 9240 8788. 33 Wheat Rd, Darling Harbour.
Hotline: T: 1800 067 676, www.sydneyvisitorcentre.com

Also check out the **Tourism New South Wales** website (www.visitnsw.com.au), and **Citysearch Sydney** (www.sydney.citysearch.com.au), both useful.

Arriving By Air

Kingsford Smith Airport ❶ 7C/❹

This is Sydney's only international airport. There are two terminals – T1 is for international traffic and

Kingsford Smith Airport has plenty of retail outlets and facilities

T2 is used for domestic arrivals and departures. www.sydneyairport.com

Bus

If your destination is Kings Cross (see p.11), Darling Harbour (see p.7) or the City (see p.7), take the door-to-door Kingsford Smith Transport/Sydney Airporter service (T: 9666 9988). Otherwise you can take a public bus to specific locations within Sydney but be warned: bus routes can be confusing to visitors. For information about fares, timetables and connections call T: 131 500 or visit www.sydneybuses.info

Taxi

If you take a taxi, there is a A$2.50 airport pickup surcharge and any tolls on top of your fare. A one-way fare to the city centre costs about A$25. The taxi rank is located at the southern end of Sydney Airport T1 (see left).

Train

The Airport Link (T: 131 500, www.airportlink.com.au) connects the domestic and international terminals to Central Station (❷ 7D) by rail. It is the cheapest and most convenient mode of transport to the city centre.

Departing every ten to 15 minutes from 5am to 12midnight, it takes 13 minutes.

Getting Around

Tickets & Fares

Call *T: 131 500* or visit *www.131500.info* for timetable and fare information for buses, trains and ferries. Under 16s and pensioners are entitled to a concessionary fare.

For getting around, the SydneyPass (*www.sydneypass.info*) offers the best value. It's valid for three, five or seven days and can be picked up on board the Explorer buses or at any CityRail ticket office, Circular Quay (see p.6) and Manly Sydney Ferry offices and Sydney Bus TransitShops.

Boat

Sydney Harbour Escapes offer four- or eight-hour boat hire for which you don't need a boat licence. They also do romantic overnight escapes. *The Pier, 594 New S Head Rd,* *Rose Bay, T: 9328 4748, www.sydneyharbourescapes.com.au*

Bus

Buses in Sydney are easy to use. The main termini are Circular Quay (❷ **3E**), Wynyard (❷ **4D**), Town Hall (❷ **5E**) and Central (❷ **7D**) railway stations. Buses for Bondi (see p.4) depart from Circular Quay and Bondi Junction train stations. If you haven't got a SydneyPass (see above), the driver will base your fare on your ultimate destination.

Explorer buses are the main tourist shuttle buses. The red Sydney Explorer takes you around the city, and the blue Bondi Explorer through

Don't forget your parking ticket

the eastern suburbs to Watsons Bay (see p.13) and Bondi Beach (see p.4). Buy your ticket on the relevant bus.
Sydney Buses: *T: 131 500, www.sydneybuses.info*
Explorer Buses: *T: 131 500, www.sydneypass.info*

Car

Hiring a car is not necessary if you are staying in town as public transport is efficient, but it may be useful if you plan to travel outside Sydney. Various rental companies have outlets at Arrivals South at the airport's International Terminal (see p.48). One of these is Avis (*T: 8374 2847*). Otherwise Bayswater Car Rental in Kings Cross (see p.11) offers cheap, no-frills car rentals (*T: 9360 3622, www.nobirds.com.au*).

Collect coins for the parking meters in popular areas such as Bondi Beach (see p.4) and the Central Business District (see p.7). At busy times (weekends for Bondi and weekdays for the city centre) it's impossible to find a parking space.

know it

Local Driving Conditions & Laws

You can drive in Sydney on a foreign licence – bring a translation with you if it's not in English. Drive on the left and wear a seat belt. The speed limit is generally 60 kms/hour, unless signposted otherwise. Look out for speed cameras, which are small grey boxes on the side of the road. It is illegal to drive while using a hand-held mobile phone and to drive with a blood alcohol content of more than one standard drink per hour. Road & Traffic Authority (RTA): *T: 132 213.*

Ferry

Circular Quay (see p.6) is the epicentre for departures to Manly (see p.4), Darling Harbour (see p.7), Watsons Bay (see p.13), Rose Bay (see p.58), Double Bay, the North Shore and Balmain. Be aware that the ferries aren't always direct and can service several of the above stops in one trip.

Take a RiverCat from Circular Quay (see p.6) if you want to travel along the Parramatta River or to Homebush Bay (for Sydney Olympic Park, see p.5). **Sydney Ferries:** *T: 131 500, www.sydneyferries.info*

Light Rail

With services running every ten minutes, the Light Rail connects Central Station to Haymarket, Darling Harbour (see p.7), Star City, Sydney Fish Market (see p.9) and the Inner West. *T: 8584 5288, www.metrotransport.com.au*

Monorail

The raised monorail circles the city, Darling Harbour (see p.7) and the Powerhouse Museum, running every

You get good views from the monorail

three to five minutes and avoiding the traffic on the roads below.
*T: 8584 5288,
www.metrotransport.com.au*

Motorbike

Rent a bike or take a tour on a Harley. **Easy Rider:** *T: 9247 2477, www.easyrider.com.au*
Blue Thunder Down Under Tours: *T: 1300 258 384, www.bluethunderdownunder.com.au*

Seaplane

See p.55.

Taxi

Catch taxis from ranks located outside railway stations and major hotels, or raise your arm to hail one. Fares start at A$2.90. Taxis are hard to catch on Friday and Saturday nights, so allow extra travelling time – especially around 3am, which is changeover time (as is 3pm).
ABC: *T: 132 522;*
Legion: *T: 131 451;*
Combined: *T: 133 300;*
Silver Service Taxis: *T: 133 100.*

It's easy to exchange currency all over Sydney

Train

CityRail trains transport you around the city and to many of the suburbs via the network's ten lines. Most do not run between 12midnight and 4.30am and instead a special NightRide bus service operates. You can use any valid CityRail ticket, or purchase a ticket from the driver. For travel outside Sydney, CountryLink provides a rail and coach service.
CityRail: T: 131 500, www.cityrail.info
CountryLink: T: 132 232, www.countrylink.info

Water Taxi

You'll find water taxis at Circular Quay (see p.6). They collect and drop you wherever you want, and do tours.

Water Taxis Combined:
T: 9555 8888,
www.watertaxis.com.au
Yellow Water Taxis:
T: 1300 138 840, www.yellowwatertaxis.com

Banks & Money

There are four major banks in Australia and they all have branches everywhere. They are: ANZ (www.anz.com); Commonwealth (www.commbank.com.au); National Australia Bank (www.national.com.au) and Westpac (www.westpac.com.au).

ATMs

Cash machines for the major banks (see above) and some of the smaller ones are on main streets around the city and its suburbs. You can also draw money at inner-city Woolworths (www.woolworths.com.au) and Coles (www.coles.com.au) supermarket registers. They accept Australian bankcards and foreign cards such as Maestro Cirrus and Plus.

Changing Money

There are facilities all over the city for changing both cash and travellers' cheques. As they charge commission, it's best to visit one of the banks, where rates are considerably lower.

Currency

The local currency is the Australian dollar (A$), which is divided into 100 cents. There is no limit on the amount of foreign or Australian currency you can bring into the country, although amounts more than A$10,000 must be declared to Customs.

Opening Times

Banks are open 9.30am-4pm, Monday to Thursday, and 9.30am-5pm on Fridays. All banks are closed on Saturdays, Sundays and public holidays (see p.54).

Climate

Sydney's average summer temperature is 23°C (about 76°F),

and its average winter temperature, 12°C (about 56°F). Visit the Commonwealth Bureau of Meteorology's website or call the hotline for five-day forecasts, T: 9296 1555, www.bom.gov.au

The best time to visit Sydney is in the autumn (between March and May) when the weather is pleasantly temperate. During summer (particularly December and January) it is busy and hot and you will need to use a high-factor sun cream.

Quarantine Laws
Australia has strict quarantine laws to shelter its unique flora and fauna. Don't bring foodstuffs, plants, soil or animals into the country. Customs x-ray your bags on the way out of the terminal so you'll be caught and fined if you do. In case you forget, bins are placed around the airport to allow you to dispose of anything that shouldn't be brought in.

Winter (June to August) will put paid to the beach but you could catch the New South Wales ski season.

Consulates

British Consulate-General ❷ 3E
1 Macquarie Pl, Circular Quay,
T: 9247 7521,
www.ukinaustralia.fco.gov.uk

Canadian Consulate General ❷ 3E
Level 5, 111 Harrington St, Sydney,
T: 9364 3000,
www.geo.international.gc.ca

New Zealand Consulate-General ❷ 4E
Level 10, 55 Hunter St, Sydney CBD,
T: 8256 2000, www.nzembassy.com

US Consulate General ❷ 4E
Level 59, MLC Centre,
19-29 Martin Pl, T: 9373 9200,
www.sydney.usconsulate.gov/sydney

Disabled Access

Disabled travellers will find Sydney well equipped for their travel needs. All the taxi companies (*see p.50*) have wheelchair-accessible vehicles – request one when booking. Trains, ferries and some bus routes have lifts and ramps – call the transport infoline (*T: 131 500*). For information on access at entertainment and eating venues, visit the Access Foundation's website (*www.accessibility.com.au*), or consult a copy of the Australian Quadriplegic Association's (AQA) Access Sydney guide by calling *T: 9281 8214*.

Electricity & Voltage

In Australia, voltage is 220/240V, 50Hz AC, using a three-pronged socket. Many hotels are fitted with 110V sockets for electric razors. Adaptors are cheap and widely available.

Emergencies

For general emergencies (fire, police, ambulance) call *T: 000*. For less urgent matters, try the Police Assistance Line: *T: 131 444*. If you have a GSM mobile and your network doesn't have reception, dial *T: 112* and your call will be carried by another GSM network. For CDMA mobiles, dial *T: 000* to be picked up by any CDMA network.

Hospitals

For Accident and Emergency departments, contact:

Royal North Shore Hospital ❶3C
Pacific Hwy, St Leonards,
T: 9926 7111.

St Vincent's Hospital ❷7G
Victoria St, Darlinghurst, T: 8382 7111,
www.svh.stvincents.com.au

Sydney Hospital ❷4F
Macquarie St, Sydney, T: 9382 7111,
www.sesahs.nsw.gov.au/sydhosp

Insurance

Although Sydney's healthcare system is relatively inexpensive, it's still sensible to include health insurance in your package.

Internet Cafés

Internet cafés are widespread, particularly down the southern end of George Street. Other places to get a connection include the State Library of New South Wales (❷4F, booking advisable, free access) at *Macquarie St, Sydney, T: 9273 1414, www.sl.nsw.gov.au*. If you have a laptop, Azure Wireless has plenty of wireless hotspots. For more information, visit the website at *www.azure.com.au*

Left Luggage

Leave your luggage at the airport with Smarte Carte in Arrivals North, *T: 9667 0926.*

Lost Property

If you lose your bags at the airport call reception on *T: 9667 9583*. For taxis, ring the relevant company (*see p.50*), and for public transport call the transport infoline at *T: 131 500*.

Personal Safety

Though relatively safe, you should still be cautious about walking Sydney's streets at night on your own, particularly in areas like Kings Cross (❷5H-6H, *see p.11*), Darlinghurst (*see p.18*) – most specifically Victoria Street (❷7G) – and the backstreets of Woolloomooloo (❷5G).

At the Beach

Always swim between the red and yellow flags at Sydney's beaches. These pinpoint the safest areas to swim and also those patrolled by lifeguards. Strong currents (rips) are prevalent at many surf beaches. If you get caught in one, stay calm, float with it and raise your hand or swim across it rather than against it. Ask lifeguards about surf conditions. The Australian sun is extreme, so always wear sunscreen. Sydney Harbour and its surrounds are home to 60 species of shark and ray. Though some, such as the tiger shark, are dangerous, beach attacks are extremely rare.

know it

Pharmacies

There aren't any 24-hour pharmacies in Sydney, and only a handful are even open on Sundays. One that does is Blakes Pharmacy: *20 Darlinghurst Rd, Kings Cross, T: 9358 6712.* Outside operating hours, contact the hospitals Emergency department (see p.53).

Post Offices

Australia Post is generally efficient. The General Post Office is located at Martin Place (❷ 4E). *Open 8.15am–5.30pm Mon-Fri, 10am-2pm Sat. 1 Martin Pl, T: 13 13 18.*

Postboxes in Sydney are hard to miss!

Public Holidays

Please note that opening times for bars, restaurants and sights may vary on public holidays.

1 Jan	New Year's Day (and the following Mon if the 1st is a weekend day)
26 Jan	Australia Day (see p.59)
Late Mar/ Apr	Easter
25 Apr	ANZAC Day (see p.60)
Mid Jun	Queen's Birthday
Early Aug	Bank Holiday (not state-wide)
Early Oct	Labour Day
25 Dec	Christmas Day
26 Dec	Boxing Day (and the following Mon if the 26th is a Sun)

Sightseeing

Opening Times

Sights in Sydney tend to open at 9.30am and close at 5pm, with last entry around 4.30pm. Note that some sights are either not open at weekends, or are only open at weekends. Check the listings in this guide, call the sight or museum itself or visit its website.

Ticket Concessions/Passes

Head to a Sydney Visitor Centre outlet (see p.48) to find out about the promotions that are on offer. The Historic Houses Trust 'Ticket Through Time' (see box, p.7) is also useful for a lesson in colonial history.

Telephones

Calls within the Sydney area are very cheap, at 40 cents per call from public telephones. Telstra (*T: 13 22 00*) has more than 4,000 public payphones, and there are other blue payphones dotted around run by smaller telecoms companies. They all take Australian coins and most of them accept credit cards and phone cards.

Codes

To call abroad from Sydney, dial 00 11 followed by the country code and then the local number, removing the first zero if there is one.

Canada 1; **Irish Republic** 353; **New Zealand** 64; **UK** 44; **USA** 1.

For calls within Sydney, just dial the number. If you're calling an Australian mobile, remove the prefix 61 (for Australia) and dial 0 before you dial 4. To call within Australia, first dial the state or territory code and then the number. Call the Operator (T: 1234) for assistance.

Mobile Phones

To avoid paying massive roaming rates, buy a 'prepaid' rechargeable card. Local network Optus has a service offering super-cheap rates to overseas landlines and mobiles, as well as reasonable local rates (❷ 6F, *Shop C, 1 Oxford St, Darlinghurst, T: 9283 7666, www.optus.com.au*). Arrange for your network at home to 'unlock' your handset so it can accept another network's SIM card.

Phone Cards

Telstra offers three types of phone card with discounted domestic and international call rates. Phone cards sell for between A$10 and A$50.

Useful Numbers

The following services are free.
Local directory enquiries: 1223; **International directory enquiries:** 1225; **Operator-assisted calls:** 1234.

To call Sydney from abroad dial Australia's country code, +61, followed by the area code 2 for Sydney.

Tours

Sydney Visitor Centre branches (see p.48) can point you in the right direction, or go direct to the Sydney Harbour National Park Information Centre (see p.11) for interesting heritage tours (T: 9247 5033). Sydney Explorer buses leave Circular Quay every 18 minutes (see p.49).

By Air

Take a seaplane around the harbour or out of town with Sydney Seaplanes: T: 1300 732 752, *www.seaplanes.com.au*, minimum price A$160, or try Sydney HeliTours' harbour tours on T: 9317 3402,

www.avta.com.au

By Boat

Masses of cruises are advertised at Circular Quay (see p.6). Try Captain Cook Cruises at T: 1800 804 843, *www.captaincook.com.au*, or Sydney Ferry cruises: T: 131 500, *www.sydneyferries.info*, which are cheaper. They operate daily with a commentary. To speed around the harbour, go for Oz Jet Boating, T: 9808 3700, *www.ozjetboating.com*

On Foot

The Visitors Information Centre is well stocked with self-guided walk brochures.

One of many boat tours around Sydney Harbour

know it

directory

This Sydney directory contains everything you need to get the best of the city, from annual events and festivals to finding the best hotels in all categories. There are suggestions for seeking out additional places of interest, a few some way from the city – none of which you will find in earlier chapters. There are also ideas for further reading, useful websites, listings and entertainment magazines and local newspapers, as well as a feature on the lingo of both Sydneysiders and Aborigines.

Key to Icons

Hotel Facilities

- Room Service
- Restaurant
- Fully Licensed Bar
- En-suite Bathroom
- @ Business Centre
- Health Centre
- ❄ Air Conditioning
- P Parking

Price Guide
(per double room)
- $ budget under A$100
- $$ moderate A$100-250
- $$$ luxury A$250-400
- $$$$ deluxe more than A$400

Places to Stay

Book rooms through the Sydney Visitor Centres (*see p.48*) or on the web. Accommodation is generally subject to GST (*see box, p.25*), and, in city-centre hotels, to a ten per cent State Government bed tax. If you're staying longer than a few days, talk to your hotel about discounted rates. Prices are based on rates for a standard double room, including the taxes and add-ons.

City Centre

Super Swish Hotels

Park Hyatt $$$$ ❷ 2E

Its harbourside position and timeless rooms make it, arguably, the best hotel in Sydney. Most of its 158 rooms, all tastefully decorated in cool tones, have private balconies overlooking Sydney Harbour Bridge.
7 Hickson Rd, The Rocks,
T: 9241 1234,
www.sydney.park.hyatt.com

The Observatory $$$$ ❷ 3D

Large rooms sporting ornate décor and luxurious marble bathrooms. Its day spa is a major draw, as is its 20-m (66-ft) indoor pool, with a ceiling whose lights represent the southern hemisphere's constellations. *89-113 Kent St, near The Rocks, T: 9256 2222, www.observatoryhotel.com.au*

The Westin Sydney $$$-$$$$ ❷ 4E

Set within the historic General Post Office Building, the Westin enjoys a solid reputation and has won several high profile international awards. Its sumptuous Heritage and Tower Rooms set it aside from many of its city-centre counterparts. *1 Martin Pl, Central Business District, T: 8223 1111, www.westin.com/sydney*

Boutique Hotels

The Establishment Hotel $$$-$$$$ ❷ 3E

Restored warehouse with minimalist, hip guest rooms. Celebrities such as Keanu Reeves have bunked down here. *5 Bridge Ln, Sydney, T: 9240 3100, www.merivale.com*

Budget

Wake Up at Central $ ❷ 7D

The best backpacker hostel in Sydney offers laundry, television, kitchen facilities and 24-hour entry. *509 Pitt St, Central, T: 9288 7888, www.wakeup.com.au*

Out of the Centre

Really Smart Hotels

Ravesi's $$-$$$$ ❶ 5F

There are 16 warm, chocolate-coloured rooms, six of which are split-level suites and most of which have panoramic views of Bondi Beach (see p.4). It was named 'the State's Hotel Bar of the Year' in 2008. *118 Campbell Pde, Bondi, T: 9365 4422, www.ravesis.com.au*

Stamford Plaza $$$ ❶ 4E, ❷ 3E

Opulent-but-elegant rooms in a National Heritage listed building. For the ultimate indulgence book the vast Presidential Suite, which has two lounge suites, a Steinway grand piano and four balconies. The heated rooftop pool also has stunning views across the bay. *33 Cross St, Double Bay, T: 9362 4455.* **Branches**: *Sir Stamford, 93 Macquarie St, Circular Quay, T: 9252 4600, www.stamford.com.au*

Boutique Hotels

The Medusa $$$ ❷ 6G

Eighteen award-winning rooms, each with a mini kitchenette. This snazzy little hotel is conveniently located in Darlinghurst, prime café country. It is the only luxury hotel to welcome dogs (2 dogs permitted per room). *267 Darlinghurst Rd, Darlinghurst, T: 9331 1000, www.medusa.com.au*

Bed & Breakfast

Bed & Breakfast Sydney Harbour $$ ❷ 2D

A fully restored heritage mansion with nine comfortable rooms each beautifully furnished and welcoming. *140-142 Cumberland St, The Rocks, T: 9247 1130, www.bedandbreakfastsydney.com*

Manly Harbour Loft $$ ❶ 2G

Light, airy rooms tinted a gorgeous sea-blue and featuring whitewashed balconies overlooking Manly's palm trees and Sydney Harbour. *12 George St, Manly, T: 9949 8487, www.manlyloft.com.au*

Tricketts B&B $$ ❶ 5C

Fully restored, Victorian mansion in the bohemian suburb of Glebe, which, with its village atmosphere and proximity to the city centre, offers a perfect base. Period furnishings and antiques add to the appeal of its four luxury en-suites. *270 Glebe Point Rd, Glebe, T: 9552 1141, www.tricketts.com.au*

Budget

Hotel Formule 1 $ ❷ 6G

Simple, functional, fixed-price accommodation for up to four people per room (make a request when booking). Conveniently located in the heart of **Kings Cross** (see p.11). It has four siblings at locations around Sydney, including the **Airport** (T: 8339 1840). *191-201 William St, Kings Cross, T: 9326 0300, www.formule1.com.au*

The Maisonette $ ❷ 4H

On buzzy Challis Avenue, this recently renovated find is simple yet comfortable. Each room is spic and span and equipped with necessities, including microwave and mini-kitchenette. *31 Challis Ave, Potts Pt, T: 9357 3878, www.maisonettehotel.com*

Vibe Hotel Rushcutters Sydney $$ ❶ 4D, ❷ 6E

Near bustling Kings Cross (see p.11) and right next to Rushcutters Bay Park, this comfortable hotel offers light, modern rooms. The rooftop pool has spectacular views of both the bay and the city. *100 Bayswater Rd, Rushcutters Bay, T: 8353 8988.* **Branches:** *88 Alfred St, Milsons Pt, T: 9955 3522; 111 Goulbourn St, Sydney, T: 8272 3300, www.vibehotels.com.au*

More Bays, Beaches & Parks

Bays

Rose Bay & Shark Island ❶ 4E

Full of yachts and fishing boats, Rose Bay is fringed by some of Sydney's most affluent suburbs. There are three golf courses nearby. Secluded Shark Island is one of Sydney Harbour's five islands – it can be reached by catching a ferry over from the Lyne Park jetty (❶ 4E).

Beaches

Balmoral ❶ 2E
Balmoral's twin beaches open on to the Middle Harbour and are loved by the locals. You'll see why as you walk along the Esplanade.

Bronte Beach ❶ 5F
'Bront-ee' is an attractive, family-oriented beach with a free beachside pool and parklands for picnics. Barbecues are also available.

Coogee Beach ❶ 6F
Coogee (pronounced 'Could-gee') is south of Bondi (see p.4) and has similar golden sands and south-easterly views.

Cronulla (Off map)
Far quieter than Bondi (see p.4) and Coogee (see above) and the only Sydney beach reachable by train.

Northern Beaches ❹
The chilled-out northern beaches include Manly (see p.4), Queenscliff, Curl Curl (famous with surfers), Long Reef, Narrabeen, Avalon, Whale Beach and Palm Beach, the latter popular with the wealthy. Visit Palm Beach in a day or spend the night at pretty Barrenjoey House.
T: 9974 4001,
www.barrenjoeyhouse.com.au.

Tamarama ❶ 5F
This little sickle moon of beach is well loved by Sydney's surfers. Be careful of the strong rip (see p.53).

Parks

Ku-ring-gai Chase National Park ❹
Sydney's largest national park covers 15,000 hectares (37,000 acres) of bush containing creeks, secluded coves, wildlife and scenic walks. Its Resolute Track offers rich Aboriginal heritage sites (see box, p.8). Open 9am-5pm daily. Kalakari Visitor Centre, Ku-ring-gai Chase National Pk, Mount Colah, T: 9472 8949,
www.npws.nsw.gov.au

Beyond Sydney

Blue Mountains (Off map)
Heritage listed and two hours west of Sydney, the Blue Mountains are famous for the Three Sisters, Jenolan Caves (some 300 of them), 300-m (984-ft) cliffs, the world's steepest railway ride and its rich Aboriginal history (see box, p.8).
www.bluemts.com.au
Take a train or drive to Katoomba and stay at luxury spa retreat Lilianfels. T: 4780 1200,
www.lilianfels.com.au

Hunter Valley (Off map)
A top wine-producing area with 70 wineries; most cellar-door tastings are free.
www.winecountry.com.au lists the wineries.
Hunter Valley Visitor Centre,
445 Wine Country Dr, Pokolbin,
T: 4990 0900.

Annual Events

January
Australia Day: A celebration of national identity with plenty of events.
www.australiaday.gov.au

Big Day Out: International and local musicians play at Sydney Showground, Homebush Bay (❻).
www.bigdayout.com

directory

59

directory

Bondi Flickerfest: A festival of short films screened at the Bondi Pavilion (❶ 4F). www.flickerfest.com.au

Sydney Festival: Sydney's biggest arts festival. Check local newspapers for details. www.sydneyfestival.org.au

February
Gay & Lesbian Mardi Gras Festival: A month-long festival whose highlight is the parade along Oxford Street (see pp.11, 18) – a feast of glitter, colour and false eyelashes. Watch out for Sleaze Ball, an all-night gay and lesbian dance event in October. www.mardigras.org.au

Chinese New Year: One of the biggest outside Asia with parades and markets around Chinatown as well as colourful dragon boat races in Darling Harbour. www.sydneychinesenewyear.com.au

April
ANZAC Day: A dawn remembrance service at the Cenotaph, Martin Place (❷ 4E) and a parade of war veterans along George Street (❷ 3E-7D).

Cracker Comedy Festival: Spanning March and celebrating all things hilarious all over the city. www.crackercomedy.com.au

Royal Easter Show ❻: A livestock parade a week before Good Friday, with events, games and rides. Sydney Showground, Homebush Bay. www.eastershow.com.au

May
Sydney Writers' Festival: More than 200 events allowing international and local writers to interact with audiences in Sydney and the Blue Mountains (see p.59). www.swf.org.au

June
Darling Harbour Jazz Festival ❸: Jazz, food and fun at Darling Harbour. www.darlingharbour.com

Sydney Film Festival: Includes shorts, animation and documentaries. www.sydneyfilmfestival.org

August
City to Surf Fun Run: Begun in 1971, this 14-km (9-mile) road race to Bondi (see p.4) now has 58,000 entrants. www.city2surf.sunherald.com.au

October
Manly Jazz Festival: Australia's largest, longest-running community-based jazz festival set against a stunning beachfront backdrop. www.manly.nsw.gov.au/manlyjazz

November
Sculpture by the Sea: International sculpture stands along the Bondi (see p.4) to Bronte (see p.59) coastline.

Melbourne Cup: Held in Melbourne, but Sydney's Randwick Race Course buzzes.

December
Carols In The Domain ❷ 4F: A free public concert for Christmas.

Open Air Cinemas: Outdoor screenings take place at various locations in Sydney from December to February. Try the screen at the Centennial Park Amphitheatre (❶ 5E) or the Royal Botanic Gardens (see pp.10-11) for harbour backdrops.

*T: 1300 366 649,
www.sydneycitysearch.com.au/section/film*

Sydney to Hobart Yacht Race: Departing Sydney on the 26th of December, this 1,010-km (128-mile) race is one of the world's most gruelling yacht races and is known as the 'Everest' of recreational races.

New Year's Eve: The Sydney Harbour fireworks display is now recognised as one of the world's best, but to grab your viewpoint – and keep it – settle in by 10am.

English-Language Newspapers

Sydney's major daily newspapers are the **Sydney Morning Herald** (*www.smh.com.au*) and the national broadsheet, **The Australian** (*www.theaustralian.news.com.au*) for in-depth analysis. More tabloid is the **Sun-Herald** (*www.sunherald.com.au*). The **Australian Financial Review** (*www.afr.com*) covers financial news.

Listings Magazines

For entertainment, get Friday's **Sydney Morning Herald** for its *Metro* supplement. Free weekly publications **Drum Media** and **3-D World** detail dance, rock and alternative music. Find them in newsagents and music stores. The free weekly **Where Magazine**, available at Sydney Visitor Centres (*see p.48*), is also helpful. Consult the **Sydney Star Observer** (official partner to the Mardi Gras (*see p.60*) *www.ssonet.com.au*) for gay and lesbian events.

Further Reading

Billington's Sydney, *Robert Billington*. This well-known photographer captures Sydney's essence in portraits and landscapes.

Down Under, *Bill Bryson*. Bryson hones in on Australia, with all his usual wit.

The Fatal Shore, *Robert Hughes*. A history of Australian colonisation.

The Sydney Morning Herald Good Food Guide, *Matthew Evans & Simon Thomsen* (eds.).

Websites

www.bom.gov.au
Detailed national weather.

www.cityofsydney.nsw.gov.au
Sydney Council's useful site includes information on accessibility.

www.oztrek.com.au
First ecological tour operator in Sydney. Offers short and long tours.

www.sydneycitysearch.com.au
Comprehensive website for venue and event listings.

www.trailfinders.com.au
Australian site, with Sydney offices. Does tours around Australia too.

www.visitnsw.com
Tourism New South Wales' website.

speak it

Australians abbreviate almost everything, so shorten your words adding 'y', 'ie', 'a' or 'o' and you'll fit right in with the locals. Australian slang also incorporates indigenous tribal words and many Aboriginal words have been immortalised as names for areas, beaches and parks.

Slang

A few roos loose in the top paddock: someone not quite there mentally.
Agro: angry, aggressive.
Ankle biter: small child.
Arvo: afternoon.
Avos: avocados.
Aussie ('Ozzie'): Australian.
Barbie ('bahbie'): barbecue.
Beaut: great.
Bikkie: biscuit, cookie.
Bloke: Australian male.
Bottle shop, bottle-o: liquor store, off-licence.
Brekky: breakfast.
Bush: the **Outback**, out of town.
Chook: chicken.
Chrissie: Christmas.
Coat hanger: Sydney Harbour Bridge.
Cozzie: swimsuit.
Daggy: dorky, unfashionable.
Daks: trousers.
Damper: bread made from flour and water.
Dinkum, fair dinkum: the real thing.
Doona: duvet, quilt.
Esky: ice box for drinks and food.
Feeling crook: feeling ill.
G'day: hello.
Good onya: good for you, well done.
Grog: alcohol.
Icy pole, ice block: popsicle, pice lolly.
Lollies: candy, sweets.
Longneck: 750 ml bottle of beer.
Macca's: McDonald's.
Mate: affectionate, informal way to address anyone from a complete stranger to your best friend.
Middy: small glass of beer.
Mozzie: mosquito.
No worries!: no problem!
Ocker: loud-mouthed Australian.
Outback: interior of Australia.
Pokies: poker machines, fruit machines, gambling slot machines.
Ripper ('rippa'): fantastic.
Roo: short for kangaroo.
Sambo: sandwich.
Schooner: large glass of beer.
Shark biscuit: surfing amateur.
Sheila: woman.
Snag: sausage.
Stubby: small bottle of beer.
Ta: thanks.
Thongs: flip flops.
True blue: patriotic.
Veggies: vegetables.
Woop Woop: a place in the middle of nowhere. *He lives in Woop Woop.*

Aboriginal Place Names

Bondi: the sound of tumbling waters.
Coogee: rotten seaweed.
Cronulla: small pink shells.
Ku-ring-gai: name of a local tribe.

index

A
Accommodation 56–58
Air travel 48, 55
Annual events 59–61
Art galleries 6, 10, 19
Art Gallery of New South Wales 10
Australian Museum 7

B
Ballet 30, 31
Banks 51
Bars 41, 43, 44–45
Beaches 4, 58–59
Birkenhead Point 22
Blue Mountains 59
Boats 49, 50, 55
Bondi Beach 4, 24
Buses 48, 49

C
Cadman's Cottage 11–12
Cafés 39, 42
Car hire 49
Chinatown 6
Cinema 28–29, 60
Circular Quay 6
Classical music 30, 31
Climate 51–52
Clubs 28
Consulates 52

D
Dance 30, 31, 34
Darling Harbour 7
Department stores 22
Disabled access 52
Domain, The 10
Drinking 41
Driving 49–50

E
Electricity 52
Elizabeth Bay House 11
Emergencies 52–53
Entertainment 26–35

F
Ferries 50

G
Gay & Lesbian events 60
Government House 10

H
Hospitals 53
Hotels 56–57, 58
Hunter Valley 59
Hyde Park 7

I
Indigenous cultures 8, 23, 34
Insurance 53
Internet 53, 61

J
Jazz 32, 60

K
Kids' venues 12
Kings Cross 11
Ku-ring-gai Chase National Park 59

L
Left luggage 53
Lost property 53
Luna Park 4

M
Malls 18, 23
Manly Beach 4
Markets 9, 24–25
Money 51
Motorbikes 50

Museum of Contemporary Art 6
Museum of Sydney 6–7
Museums 6–7, 8
Music 30–31, 32–33, 34, 60
Musicals 32

N
National Maritime Museum 8
Newspapers 61
North Head 12

O
Opals 24
Opening hours 51, 54
Opera 30
Oxford Street 11

P
Pharmacies 54
Post 54
Public holidays 54
Public transport 48–49, 50

Q
Quarantine Station 12
Queen Victoria Building 8

R
Restaurants 36–44
Rock & pop 32–33
Rocks, The 13, 25
Rose Bay 58
Royal Botanic Gardens 10–11

S
Safety 53
St Mary's Cathedral 8–9
Shark Island 58
Shopping 9, 16–25

Smoking 41
Sport & activities 5, 33–35, 60–61
Sydney Aquarium 9
Sydney Fish Market 9
Sydney Harbour Bridge 4
Sydney Observatory 12
Sydney Olympic Park 5
Sydney Opera House 5–6, 29–30
Sydney Tower 9–10
Sydney Wildlife World 9

T
Taronga Zoo 12–13
Tax 25
Taxis 48, 50
Telephones 54–55
Theatre 30, 31–32
Tickets 32, 49
Tipping 39
Tourist information 48, 61
Tours 55
Trains 48, 49, 50

V
Vaucluse 13
Vaucluse House 13

W
Water taxis 51
Watsons Bay 13

Whilst every care has been taken to check the accuracy of the information in this guide, the publishers cannot accept responsibility for errors or omissions or the consequences thereof. No part of this guide may be reproduced without the permission of the publishers.
Published by
Compass Maps Ltd.
info@popoutmaps.com
www.popout-travel.com
© 2009 Compass Maps Ltd.
Written by Tamsin Bradshaw.
Updated by Darroch Donald.
Revision management by Cambridge Publishing Management Ltd.
Pictures © Compass Maps Ltd and Susannah Sayler.
Cover images: AW Photography-Commercial Alamy and Wiskerke/Alamy.
This PopOut product, its associated machinery and format use, whether singular or integrated within other products, is subject to worldwide patents granted & pending, including
EP1417665,
CN ZL02819864.6 &
CN ZL200620006638.7.
All rights reserved including design, copyright, trademark and associated intellectual property rights. PopOut is a registered trademark and is produced under licence by Compass Maps Ltd.

8085